CHOICES

CHOICES

BY

ANDREW GORDON SIMS

DORRANCE PUBLISHING CO., INC.
PITTSBURGH, PENNSYLVANIA 15222

ISBN # 0-8059-6055-4

Printed in the United States of America

First Printing

For information or to order additional books, please write:
Dorrance Publishing Co., Inc.
701 Smithfield Street, Fifth Floor
Pittsburgh, Pennsylvania 15222
U.S.A.
1-800-788-7654
Or visit our web site and on-line catalog at *www.dorrancepublishing.com*

To my mother,
Helen McNeely Sims,
who has always been my favorite teacher.

Hey, what's going on? I see a hospital room. A doctor is reading a chart. I hear the nurse cry out. "Doctor! Come quick. We are losing him!"

What the—well, I'll be....It's true. I can see myself on the table. So there is something to this light you're supposed to see after death! Now what? Maybe when all my brain cells die, I'll stop this hallucinating.

I gotta admit this is much better than lying on the table. Boy, here I am floating like a cloud! Look at those people working to revive me. Man, look at the buns on that nurse! Oh, shake shake shake, shake your bootie. Tell me you want me, sweetie. That's why you are working so hard. Yeah, you want to save me for yourself.

Hey, where's everyone going? Oops, looks like I didn't make it, but man, I'm still here! Why haven't I faded into the sunset? This is really strange. Maybe I'm going to be a ghost. Yeah, like Casper. Yeah, and I can watch all the girls take showers. I feel like Kevin Bacon in *Hollow Man*. What a nasty little boy I can be! Surely I'm not going to be the operating room ghost, hanging around up here watching other people die. What a drag! This is starting to bite.

"Hello, is anybody home?" I hear a noise like a train at top speed.

What the—where am I? That blinding light is so bright I can't take it. What kind of room is this? Why am I sitting in this chair? I don't think I like this. "Hello, is anybody home? Jees, you scared the devil out of me!"

A man wearing a purple robe with a black sash is standing in front of me saying, "I don't think so." His skin is pale gray. He looks like a Greek statue, and his eyes are cold looking. There is no emotion on his face.

"What the hell does that mean? Who are you? Where did you come from?"

The man speaks again. "I am the Governor GEDOONS, he who eliminates your name. You've got a big mouth. We can use a smart guy like you in our PR department. As of this moment, your name has been removed."

Someone speaks out. "I am the Governor ZAXANIN, he who names things. As of today you have a new name and a new title. Since you're not too bright, they will be the same. Your new name/title is Pervert."

"To hell with—"

Suddenly the sound of a train passes right on top of me, and then....

Where am I? Hey, this is more like it. A bar!

Without looking up, the bartender asks. "What'll you have?"

"I'll have a bourbon. Yeah, things are looking up. For a moment I thought I was in deep—man, that's the best bourbon I've ever had. How about another?" Instantly a line of drinks all the way to the end of the long bar appears.

This must be my lucky day. "Well, don't mind if I do. Yes, I'll have another one. Oh, sure I'll be glad to join you. Well, it would be a shame to let all this great booze go to waste. Wait a minute. Wait a minute. Why am I not getting a buzz? What kind of bourbon is this? Not only am I not getting drunk, I don't even need to go to the boy's room.

Then a voice booms, "Everyone, move back! Kerubic Angels are approaching." Four beings come through the wall. Not the door, but the wall. They look like the creature from that old Sinbad movie, the Cyclops or something, but with two eyes and wings. Man, they sure don't look friendly. One of them has the name ABOZ on his forehead. They don't seem to see me. I'm getting out of here.

Then someone announces, "Stand aside for AIRA, the Servient Angel, and companions that comprehend the Species and Uses of the Living Creatures in each of the Four Elements."

Man, this thing called AIRA looks equally bad to the bone. There's going to be trouble. I don't think these guys like each other. The bartender is turning white. Man, these beings look ticked. This looks like something out of *Star Wars*. Oh, man!

A tremendous flash of light and....

Man, that hurts.

Abruptly somehow I am transported to this room. It resembles a judge's chamber. There is a large desk that comes up to my nose. Behind the desk are two beings.

"Who are you guys?"

One of them speaks. "I am the Governor TEDOOND, he who demands obedience."

TEDOOND is in a black and white robe. He is wearing a belt instead of a sash like the other governors. The belt looks to be of leather and has a buckle made of leather also. There is a mark on the buckle, but I can't make it out.

Someone speaks. "I am The Calvary Cross Angel NOALMR, he who is first to bring about torment." This being has the color and texture of iron. His wings look like the wings of a large vulture, but the edges are filed down to a razor-sharp edge. They look like the edge of a sword, but are all the way around the outer fringe of the wings. In his right hand is a sword that appears to be made out of the same material as his wings. On his left hand is a glove with spikes that look like polished silver. He is extremely muscular and scary.

"Is this some kind of joke?"

"Do you know what pain is?" asks NOALMAR.

"Of course, you idiot."

TEDOOND barks, "What name were you given?"

"None of your—Oh, my God!" What pain! "Help me! Someone help me!"

NOALMR speaks. "When you are asked your name or title, you will give the one you were given or feel the pain."

"What is your name?" asks TEDOOND.

'Pervert."

The pain stops.

"Where are we?"

TEDOOND answers, "We are in a holding shuttle. We will be here until you are prepped for your assignment."

"What assignment?"

"You are in public relations, Pervert."

"What kind of public relations?"

"Actually, you have been chosen to be an Eluder."

"Yeah, right, I'm an Eluder."

"Yes, you are an Eluder, and you have been rewarded."

"Rewarded for what?"

"You are being rewarded for serving your master."

"What master?"

"Satan."

"You must be crazy. I'm nobody's servant. Ooh, God! What pain! Help me! Please help me!"

"Why are you calling God's name?" asks NOALMR. "You are not one of His. You didn't follow Him or His Word, so why do you call out to Him? How sad."

TEDOOND roars, "We are running out of time. You have been chosen because you have a big mouth and sham tongue. If you prefer, you can be sent with the others. I don't care. You don't have to be an Eluder."

At that moment, a vision appears among them of Hell at. its core. The people are so hot, some of them break out in flames and beat themselves with their hands to put out the flames. Most of them have what looks like ringworms under their skin. The worms are bursting through from time to time and creating a lot of pain. All of them are weeping and begging for mercy. The looks on the faces of the people are so sad, I can't describe them. All I can do is grimace in reaction to what I am seeing.

"How long do I get to be an Eluder?"

"Until the final war.

I know enough to know that in the final war God wins.

The Calvary Cross Angel OBAUA, he who has half of truth, says, "That's the plan. Our master has a bit of a surprise for you know who. He has some Dark Angels planted in the Kingdom, and at the very moment when Jesus is to descend and rule the earth, our angels are going to kill Him. I'm told that the only time Jesus is vulnerable is when He is descending down from the Kingdom to earth. This is why our lord was thrown out of Heaven. God cast out our master because Satan would have killed Jesus and claimed his rightful place.

"What do you mean, his rightful place?"

"Satan was to be the Word. He was to be the one to sit next to God. Then his brother Jesus betrayed him. He told his Father that Satan had formed a group to try and take over the Kingdom. He said that our lord was plotting to overthrow God Himself So God had a trial. The trial in human time lasted for approximately 12,333 years. After the trial, all of Heaven was divided. Most of the Kingdom sided with Jesus because they felt no one would make something up like that about their brother. God was so bewildered by what happened, He created a scenario with two humans to recreate the potential of a brother betraying the other (Cain and Abel).

"Satan was cast down here and denied his rightful place at the right hand of God. This is not over. When our lord was cast out of the kingdom, he didn't lose his power. He is still the lord of the earth. If you think that what we are telling you is not true, then consider who has the power on earth. It is not Jesus, but our lord. Why? Because he is the second most powerful entity in the universe. Only God is more powerful, but our lord's power is growing. When the time is right, Jesus has but one chance to dethrone our lord. He will have to leave heaven and descend to earth to try to capture our armies with His. In order to do that, He must use all of His forces. All of his power.

"Wait a minute, wait a minute. Even I know that God is all powerful. Give me a break. How could anything overcome God?"

"Well, since God is all powerful and Jesus is at His right hand, how can anything defeat them? That's a fair question. If God is all powerful and Jesus is too, then why have a war? Why haven't they already destroyed our lord? Where are they? Why would a 'loving,' all powerful God let everyone go through all this refuse? Why wouldn't He crush our lord? At least bind him so that everyone would love Jesus and follow him?

"We know you're not the sharpest knife in the drawer, but surely you can see that something doesn't make sense. If Jesus was all powerful like our master, why was He persecuted? Why was He put to death? How sad, that people are worshiping the wrong lord. Jesus was a loser. He came to earth to try and overcome our lord. The only mistake our lord made was allowing Jesus to ascend back to the kingdom. Our lord thought if he let Jesus go back to the Father, then God might see who was really the heir to the throne. Now it looks as though there is no other way for our lord to receive his rightful place other than by destroying his brother. This will be regrettable because this is not what our lord wanted, but he has been given no other choice. He must destroy his brother or be exiled. Last, if our lord is not all powerful, then why did you come here? Why aren't you up there stating your case? You are here because our lord is all powerful and you have been given the opportunity to serve him."

"If I choose to serve him as an Eluder, how long do I serve, and what happens when it's over? I mean, where do I go after I'm through serving?"

TEDOOND answered, "You can serve our lord as an Eluder for as long as you would like or until the Great War. You can request to leave anytime you want. If you don't serve at all, you go where you just visited. If you serve for an eon, you will be given the title of Demon. Demons are of the highest order in the fallen human caste, but one under the rule of the Dark Angels. The Dark Angels descended from the kingdom with our lord. As an Eluder, once you have served one eon, you will have a staff that will cater to your every need. You will possess six women who are designed for your pleasure alone and six male servants to carry all of your possessions. All subjects of our lord will be required to bow when you are in their presence."

OBAUA adds, "You may change any of the women anytime you desire. We have noticed that you seem to like women who are often of a color other than your own. Here that is perfectly acceptable. We are not racists like our lord's brother. We have also noticed that you have thought of the possibilities of homosexual relationships."

"That's bull, you're crazy, you piece of..."

"Wait, we are only telling you this observation in case you want to pursue it. It is acceptable here. You can pick your male servants for any reason you desire."

"When must I give you my decision?"

"Now."

"You mean you won't give me a little time to think it over?"

TEDOOND bellows, "You know what the answer is. We need every Eluder on the front lines, winning souls. It's your choice, but you must make it now. As a matter of fact, a Seraph, one of our highest Dark Angels, is drawing near. Maybe you should go with the others. I suppose that's...."

"No, wait, I want to be an Eluder. I mean, I know I don't want to go there. Okay. Count me in. Twelve servants can't be all bad."

'Okay, here is what is going to happen. You will be with another Eluder for two battles. You will not be allowed to talk in the first one. The second is one in which you can participate. After that you are on your own."

"You mean I will only see two battles before I will be on my own? Do I get a sword or a gun'?"

"It is not that kind of battle. It is a battle of words, thoughts."

"Well, that's a relief. At least I'm not going to get blown to bits."

"No, all you are going to do is what you do best: Run your mouth, Pervert. You are just going to convince people to have a great time. To enjoy themselves. The Ghost of Light will be trying to convince them to walk with Jesus. Can you imagine? How much easier can it be? You are the one telling them to party down, and some creep is telling them to go home and kneel by their bedside and pray. You tell us, who's the A Team?"

OBAUA says, "Well, Pervert, you are about to leave us. Goodbye and to Hell with you."

They laugh.

"Bite me, you jerks. God, what is that light?" The sound of thunder is all around. Where am I? All of a sudden I'm in an office with several people standing around.

"Okay, Pervert, don't speak." It's an Eluder speaking right next to me. The Eluder roars, "If you speak, the pain you felt before will be like foreplay compared to what will happen to you here. The guy in white is the Ghost of Light. We, in case you didn't notice, are in black."

The Eluder continues, "The battlefield is the orb. There are people around, but the victim is the one in the center of the orb. We are at one position, and the Ghost is at the other. You will talk to the victim's subconscious as though you were engaging him in conversation. You and the Ghost are his thoughts. Not the total sum of all his thoughts, but you are inputting into his thought process."

"Where do I stand?"

"You will levitate above but behind me."

Then all at once all the voices in the office are audible.

"Jerry," Sherry asks, "you mean your wife won't understand if you go with us for just one drink?"

"No, Sherry. She doesn't have a sense of humor."

The Eluder asks. "Jerry, what's the big deal? They like you. They just want to spend a little time with you. Especially Sherry. She's kinda cute."

Then the Ghost speaks. "Jerry, your wife would be proud if she could see you now. Hang in there."

Bill asks, "Jerry, have you ever played any pool?"

"Yeah, Bill, I told you the other day that I used to shoot pool when I was in college."

"Well, Jerry, I don't want to hurt your feelings, but I'm about the best pool player I ever saw.

"Bill, you couldn't hit a bull in the butt with a bass fiddle."

Everyone laughs.

"Well, Jerry, if you think you can handle it, come on down."

It is obvious that Bill has a thing for Sherry but is getting nowhere, so he decides to try to help Sherry lure Jerry to the party, hoping to improve his posture with her at a later time.

"Do you really care what that little punk thinks, Jerry?" asks the Ghost.

The Eluder declares, "But it would be nice to shut him up in front of everyone."

Then Jerry's thoughts become audible. "Hey, I don't have to prove anything to this guy. Can't wait to see little Amy's face today. I've been waiting to hear more about her and her dad."

The Eluder quickly conveys, "Jerry, all these guys are going to think you're a sissy. Get a grip. You've got to do something, or you're going to get a negative image at the ol' workplace."

Jerry jumps up out of his chair and gathers his things and with a smile says, "See you guys Monday."

The Eluder storms, "What is that all about'? A man with no guts! What am I supposed to do about that, a man with no guts?"

The Eluder's face turns a shade darker, and it looks as though his skin right under his eye actually melts a little. Boy, what a weird sight. There is so much tension in the room you can cut it with a knife. The Ghost and the Eluder are taking into account everything that is going on. As Jerry is walking to his car, he is still the center of the orb. Both the Ghost and the Eluder are observing him and making remarks. Jerry is shaking his head, but keeps on walking. The Eluder spins around screaming, "You could've had her, you idiot. All you had to do was show up at the party and she was yours. You can sleep with Amy anytime, dope."

The Ghost just smiles. He says nothing while the Eluder rants and raves on and on.

"Okay, I'm ready for a break. I guess that one didn't go so well?" I ask.

The Eluder wheels around, and at the same time it feels as though someone has run me through with a sword. My body is on fire. I'm so weak, I think I'm going to faint.

The voice of NOALMR clamors, "Who told you to speak, Pervert? You were told not to speak on the first battle and you spoke. Now feel the pain for your lack of obedience."

Oh, God, the pain is unbearable! "Just let me die! Please let me die!"

"You idiot," the Eluder utters, "you are already dead. Oh, by the way, you don't get breaks here, Pervert. It's twenty-four on and zero off, and if you don't like it, tell it to Jimmy Hoffa. Just get on the elevator and press down. He is waiting for you. He is really hot about it, mad as hell." NOALMAR shrieks with laughter.

"Hold on. So you are saying I will be assigned to one person and I stay with him or her all the time?"

"Hey, we're politically correct around here, so you will always be with a guy. If your guy dies or gets salvation, then you will be reassigned. Sometimes some of these rookie preachers run us out. If that happens, you might end up close to Vegas for a little while until the guy lightens up, then you can take two Fiends and the three of you can have a party. The reason for the two Fiends is you must be doing something wrong if they go for the Jesus thing, so our lord is sending reinforcements.

"The thing is, our lord doesn't like to lose. So every time you lose a battle, he wants you to feel as bad as he does, so he inflicts you.

"What do you mean, inflicts' me?"

"Well, most of the time you get some reminder of the battle, just as you would when you were on earth. If you lost a battle, you would most certainly have scars from your wounds. This helps you remember how important it is to win."

"What kind of scars?"

"Usually some of your new body is dissolved, and if your presentation wasn't up to his standards, you'll find yourself with soiled pants, but you won't be able to do anything about it because you must continue the battle."

"What are the chances I could just go to Satan and ask him to kill me and get it over with?"

"One real deal breaker there. You are already dead."

"You mean there is nothing else? I'm stuck here for however long with...."

"You are here for eternity, Pervert. Forever!"

"What kind of choice is that? Why don't I have a say in where I go?"

"Hey. I don't know your life story, so forgive me for not understanding. I guess you never saw a Bible?"

"Of course I saw a Bible. I even went to church a few times. Man, I didn't have anything in common with those people, so I got out of there and never looked back."

"Well, that's the ticket, Pervert. That's why we are having this conversation. You got out of there and never looked back. And you said you had no say in coming here. See how just a little jogging of the memory brings it back."

"Bull! It wasn't my fault. If I had been shown the right way, then maybe I would have gone in another direction.

"You know, Pervert, you're just another whiner. Poor you. Nobody told her. She was mistreated," mocks the Eluder.

"Kiss my....God, help me, the pain, the pain!"

"I guess with that big mouth you just said whatever you wanted to up there. Well, you aren't up there, and you will be obedient or pay the price. You see, Missy, we don't put up with all that rebellion down here. We created rebellion. We sure as hell aren't going to tolerate it. Remember, Pervert, as long as your big mouth is of some service to our lord, he will use you. When it is of no further use, our lord will dismiss you."

"I thought I was going to get servants and be treated as royalty."

"That is only if you produce. How can you produce when all you do is whine? I think our lord will be sending you down soon. Years ago people were hard workers. Now you all think you have been mistreated. Poor little baby. If you can't afford the ticket, don't board the train. You want the servants, then get on the front line and kick butt and take names. No mercy."

"When can I see some of…?"

"Shut up! Something is happening."

Just then, the cell phone starts to ring in Jerry's car.

It's Amy. She is going shopping with the girls and won't be home for about three hours.

The Eluder smiles. "Jerry, why go home to an empty house? Let's go over to the party and show Little Bill how to play some eight ball. Let's kick some serious butt. Come on."

"That ball game is on," the Ghost responds. "You can probably watch the whole game before Amy gets home. You, a little self time."

"One time on that table, and I'll bet big mouth Bill won't ever be able to face anyone at the office again," suggest the Eluder.

Jerry swings off the side of the road and turns around, then says, "What the hell, let's shoot some pool."

"Remember, Jerry, when it was Paula?" the Ghost recalls. "You were just about ready to pop the question, and you and the boys decided to rock the town. Boy, can't forget that look on Paula's face when she opened the door and there you were, drunk and stupid! You said that was your last night of impressing the boys. But what the hey, shutting Bill's mouth is worth Amy giving you that look. After all, she's your wife. She will understand how important Bill is." Jerry slams on the brake and turns back toward home.

"Jerry, Jerry," the Eluder beseeches, "you don't have to get drunk. Just kick ol' Bill's butt! I'll bet we could do it in less than an hour and be home in time for the second half."

Jerry breaks out into, "Amy, what you gonna do? I think I'm in love with you. Falling in and out of love with you."

The Eluder shrieks, "No! No!"

I see his face melting under his right eye. What is that smell? Oh, yeah, I better not mention that. He looks pretty ticked.

The Eluder is ranting and raving now. "Amy's a whore. She's just another whore, you idiot. We could be at the party, but Super Sissy wants to be home when Amy gets there."

Jerry is going into the house, changing into his warm-ups, gets his Dr. Pepper and chips, gabs the remote control, and kicks back. Just Jerry and the game.

Watch out, Jerry, it looks like those eyes are going to shut.

"Okay, he's out for a while." The Eluder inquires, "Any questions?"

"Yes. Has anybody ever escaped this place?" I ask.

"No. There is a great chasm between the Kingdom and us. We can't get over there, and they can't get over here."

"Is there anything a person can do to earn his way out of here? Like a good deed or service rendered?"

"No. You came here because this is where you belong. You lived your life on the earth as we all did, and at your death, you were sent to the place you chose."

"Wait a minute, I didn't choose this place!"

"Of course you did. You don't think that as all knowing as God and Satan are that a mistake was made? In the book of life it says let's see, where is it? Oh here it is:

> Romans 6:1 6–18: *Don't you realize that you choose your own master? You can choose sin ('with death) or else obedience (with acquittal). The one to whom you offer yourself—he will take you and be your master and you will be his slave. Thank God that though you once chose to be slaves of sin, now you have obeyed with all your heart the teaching to which God has committed you. And now you are free from your old master, sin; and you have become slaves to your new master, righteousness.*

"It goes like this, Pervert. You had choices when you were there. You choose to believe in God or to follow the easier path."

"I didn't choose. I never knew enough to make a clear choice," I lament.

"Let's see. You never knew enough. So those times you went to church, you chose to laugh at the preacher the next day at work. Remember telling all your buddies at the bar what a loser the preacher was? Oh, yeah, remember how you told them about how poorly dressed he was? The man had no idea what a color palette was. Not to mention the limp he had. I believe you said, 'If that's the best God can do, I'll pass'."

"Hey, that's a cheap shot. I was just jerking around with my friends," I offer.

"Bad choice, Bubba. Remember Tommy Cozart? You spent the night with him when you were a senior in high school. He idolized you. Boy, was he proud to have you come over to his house after his father was killed in that tragic accident. His mother was devastated, so she drank a lot. Not only did you sleep with her that night, but you went back quite often."

"Okay, I know that was a rotten thing to do. I have regretted that forever. If I could take it back, I would."

"Bad choice, hey, mate? Did you drop to your knees and ask God to forgive you?"

"No, but I felt so bad I said many times to myself, *If I get the chance to make it up to him, I will.*"

"Did you make it up to him?"

"No."

"Looks like another bad choice. What about your first wife? Did you make a covenant with her and this God you weren't impressed with? Did you take a vow saying till death do you part, in God's holy name, and then commit adultery and break every vow you made?"

"Yes, but that was in my youth. I was just starting out. I thought it was the right thing to do at the time. Look, man, half of all marriages end up in divorce in today's world."

"Nobody made you wed the girl. Nobody made you break the covenant with God. Sounds like another bad choice. Remember that job you had at Mr. Koop's grocery? Man, that guy really liked you. He trusted you, too. You stole money from the cash register almost every day you worked there. Once you started stealing, I don't think you gave Mr. Koop one honest day's work for one honest day's pay."

"Enough! I loved that old man. He was so good to me."

"You sure had a strange way of showing your gratitude. More bad choices."

The Eluder continues, "Remember when Mark Johnson told you about the secret meeting with the boss and how he was going to get the promotion? That guy was bursting with pride. He just had to tell someone, and he thought he could trust you. That was a great lesson for him. Thanks to you pointing out to the boss how untrustworthy Mark was, he knows he can't trust anyone."

"Hey, at the time, I thought I was doing the right thing. Mark was told not to tell anyone about the promotion. I was just pointing out to the boss that Mark wasn't able to follow his instructions."

"You're a real noble dude. Bad choice."

"Do you suppose I was the only one to make some mistakes? You mean God couldn't have forgiven me for those sins?"

"Let's see, Pervert. The real question is, did you ask Him to forgive you?"

"I didn't ask him, but I was sorry for the wrong I did."

"Another bad choice."

"How in the Hell was I supposed to know what God expected of me? I mean, if there would have been a sign or something telling me what God expected…."

"How about, He put an owner's manual on every nightstand of every motel room that you took those whores to. Remember the girls from Albany that you and the guy played with? The girls leaped on one bed, and you and pokeman hit the other bed. If you would have read the owner's manual, you would have known that was a no-no."

"Well, I didn't read it, so He can't count that against me."

"That's where you little sniveling brats are so wrong. God made the rules and put them in a book in plain view for all to see. You chose not to read it. That was another bad choice. You see, baby, God doesn't care what your opinion is. You don't get a vote. All you got was an opportunity and you blew it. Now you think because the world was willing to listen to you whine about the injustices done to you that God will listen. What an idiot! A self-absorbed idiot! This is why you are here. God doesn't take the proud. He only takes the humble. Those who demand their own ways are left to themselves."

"This is so wrong. A God of mercy could not be so indifferent. He could not leave me without a hearing. Surely He will listen to my plea."

"Oh, you will get your day when Jesus descends to the earth and the final battle comes. After all is over, you will stand before Jesus."

"See, I knew I would get my chance to make my plea. Man, you sure know how to scare the fool out of me." I gulp.

"I wouldn't start knitting that white robe just yet. You see, in that manual I was talking about, Jesus said something pretty important in Matthew 7:13:

> *Heaven can be entered only through the narrow gate! The highway to hell is broad, and its gate is wide enough for all the multitudes who choose the easy way. But the gateway to life is small, and the road is narrow, and only a few ever find it.*

"What kind of perversion is this? You are an Eluder, and you are quoting the Bible?"

"In that manual you never bothered to read, well, it explains that the demons know who God is, too. When Jesus cast out our demons, do you not think they knew who He was? They called out his name. That's right, Pervert, even the demons are smart enough to acknowledge Jesus. Yet the politically correct of your time are too proud to call His name. For that, let us give thanks. We need people, too," the Eluder smiles.

"Surely, I'm going to wake up. Then all of this will be a nightmare."

"Ahhhh, poor baby."

"What does someone have to do to get to heaven?"

"Well, it's really hard. Even though you didn't read the manual, you probably know the answer. All a person has to do is believe that Jesus is the Son of God and that He died on the cross for his sins.

"And?"

"That's it, wise guy. Apparently, the acceptance of Jesus as their Lord and Savior is enough to get them into heaven."

"Yeah, well, what if they sin? What then?"

"It doesn't make any difference if they have one sin or thousands, they are forgiven and washed clean by the blood of Jesus."

"That is the dumbest thing I've ever heard. That's too easy! Anyone would do that, knowing what the chances are. You don't have to go to Vegas to figure that out."

"You didn't figure it out, Pervert," the Eluder howls.

"I don't want to talk about it anymore. It's just so crazy. Nobody in their right mind could buy into that scam."

"You're right, Pervert. How could I have been so stupid as to think you would fall for that? Why don't you just wake up and get on with your life?"

"I plan on it, Eluder. I guess this is one of those dreams that seems as though it goes on forever."

"Well, maybe this will help wake you up!" scowls the Eluder.

In a moment the Eluder's hand becomes a claw like that of a lion. He extends his hand and rips my chest open.

"Oh, God, what pain! I'm bleeding to death! I'm bleeding to death! Do something!"

"Wake up, Pervert. Call out to your mommy. God can't hear you down here. Ha ha! Did you fall out of the chair? What are you doing? Get off the floor. Wake up from your little dream, Pervert."

"I can't breathe."

"Yeah, if you were alive, that would have killed you. If you were asleep, that would have brought you back to consciousness. So I guess we can rule out both of those possibilities."

"I can't breathe!"

"That's because your lung is hanging out. Don't worry, though. You aren't going to die. You see, in spite of your big mouth, you are going to live forever, right here with the rest of us. So get used to it, Pervert."

Suddenly darkness is falling on the area. There is a presence that makes the hair on my back stand on end. Then a voice speaks. Out of the darkness appears the Governor LAPARIN, he who is the protector of man. "He is of no use to us with his lung ripped out. He can't provide proper argument. Strike him again and feel my wrath, Eluder."

"Sorry, LAPARIN. He's such a loser, it's hard to not injure him, my lord."

The extreme darkness moves past.

"Oh, God, I've been healed! I've been healed!"

"God has nothing to do with it. You're lucky a governor was passing by at the time of your unfortunate accident."

"Unfortunate accident, my....

"Maybe you would like to go two out of three?"

"Please, please, don't hurt me again."

"That's better, Pervert. Now, see if you can shut your big mouth for a while.

"I'll bet you thought healing was only done by the righteous. You and the rest of your kind. Don't feel alone, Pervert. Even those phony preachers you heard as you flipped by on those TV stations are feeling all warm and cozy. But if they were really looking at that manual, they would have seen in Matthew 7:21–23,"

> *Not all who sound religious are really godly people. They may refer to me as "Lord," but still won't get to heaven. For the decisive question is whether they obey my Father in heaven. At the judgment many will tell me, "Lord, Lord, we told others about you and used your name to cast out demons and to do many other great miracles." But I will reply, "You have never been mine. Go away, for your deeds are evil."*

"Amy's home! Back to the orb," says the Eluder.

"Jerry, Honey, isn't it hard to see who's winning with your eyes closed?" asks Amy.

"Come here, you little rascal," snickers Jerry.

"No way, Jose. You'll have to come and get me like a man."

"That does it!"

"Help! Help! Ahhhhhh. Stop, Jerry, stop before I wet my pants."

"Say 'I'm sorry, honey," demands Jerry.

In a very low voice, Amy replies, "I'm sorry."

"What was that? I didn't hear you. Did you say something?"

"I'm sorry, my big bad master."

"That's better, pipsqueak."

"They make me sick!" screeches the Eluder. "I'd like to barbecue them both on a grill and eat their flesh."

Man, the Eluder is one sick guy "No! No! How could you make me go in my pants? That's so cute," I mimic.

"One more word from you and I'll make you eat some rotten flesh, Pervert."

The Eluder exhorts, "Jerry. Tell Amy about the party Sherry wanted you to attend. Come on, she'll get a kick out of it and she will find out what a loyal guy you are. How else is she going to know what you go through just to be with her?"

"You're a good man, Jerry. Amy doesn't need to know about that," cautions the Ghost. "It would only create stress. She would always worry about what is going on at the office."

"Don't tell her about Sherry, just tell her about Bill and the pool challenge. She might even say you should have shown that jerk who the man is," barks the Eluder.

Jerry says, "Come here and let's snuggle up, baby."

"Okay, honey."

'Ah, they're going back to sleep," the Eluder notes.

The Eluder's hand is shaking as some of his skin around his fingers is badly melting. It looks as though his fingers are almost webbed.

"Any questions, Pervert?"

"So this guy—Jerry—I guess he is on his way to heaven?"

"To the contrary, Jerry is a very honorable man. He's honest, noble, trustworthy, loyal. He is the straight arrow. But if Jerry dies tonight, suddenly, without notice, he will be right here with us, Pervert."

"How can that be? I thought the whole thing was to be a straight arrow and you get in. What crazy kind of formula does it take to get to heaven? Man, this guy doesn't cheat on his wife! He doesn't cheat at work! What kind of junk is this? Is this some kind of trick? No one really gets in. Right?"

"Well, Pervert, you're close. Only the few get in."

"What few get in? You mean the saints? The ones who never commit a sin?"

"Everyone sins."

"Well, then who?"

"Well, the truth is, God has His own private little club. To belong to His club, as with any order, you must have standards, an oath, a motto. All those things. For example, one must have rules. One of the rules is you must believe that Jesus is the Son of God. Not just *say* He is the Son, but *believe* He is the Son of God. Another rule is you must believe Jesus was born of the Virgin Mary and walked the earth. Another rule is you must believe that Jesus died on the cross for your sins."

"And?"

"That's pretty much it."

"Wait a minute! Just a minute! How can that be it? How can just believing He was born of Mary and is the Son of God and died on the cross for sins be enough?"

"Well, Pervert, I'll have to admit, God is a lot smarter than I gave Him credit for when I first came here. You see, He has a test built in that assures Him there will be no phonies allowed."

"And how is that?"

"Well, the problem is, if you don't really believe, then you won't act like it. Let me try and explain it. You see, I love the way the dude does it. Boy, did He screw us—I mean the ones who wanted to go to heaven but didn't want to pay the price. Check this out—if you don't really believe but don't want to take any chances, like a lot of people, what do you do?"

"You tell me."

"You fake it. You pretend. That way if there's something to it, you'll stand a good chance of getting it, too. So you go to church every Sunday and take Bible studies so you are right there with everybody else. So if anything miraculous happens, you will be included. Of course, the problem is, the litmus test is how does that person act when they're not at church or at Bible study or with Christian friends? So all of these people are trying to do what is right. They want to be included if something great is going to happen in the church, but when they are not at the church they are their true selves. That means they do all the things that other people call them a hypocrite for, like going to the bar after work and drinking too much; talking junk to the opposite sex; lying on their tax return; criticizing their spouse; mistreating their children; being lazy and not pulling their load; being ugly to their neighbors, their parents, and in-laws; not listening to the people who need them; talking too much. The worst of all is pride. God hates little people with big egos. When He lists what He dislikes, He lists pride and haughtiness first."

"I thought all you had to do was believe in Jesus."

"That's right, Pervert. The trick is, if you really believe, then it changes your life."

"So people who believe in Jesus don't sin anymore?"

"Yeah, I think some of them sin more after they are saved than they did before."

"Hey, hey, I can only take so much of this. You just said that if they believed in Jesus that it changed their lives,"

"Crazy? Well, there have been a lot of Christians who were walking with the Lord, and the next thing you know, one of our very own Eluders talked them into one of their favorite sins. Ahhh, the sweet smell of victory! Then one of two things happens. They can't forgive themselves and turn their back on God, or they fall to their knees and beg God to forgive them. Boy, I hate it when they do that. As long as they sincerely ask God's forgiveness in Jesus' name, they're back in the saddle again. Bummer."

"You mean someone can have an affair and run home, drop on their knees, and ask for forgiveness, and everything is okay?"

"No, but someone can have an affair and truly realize they have offended God, go home and weep, fall on their knees and beg God for forgiveness, and mean it with all their heart, then God would forgive them. But if they are just covering the bases, it won't work."

"If they are sincere, would they still go to heaven?"

"Yes."

"You mean to tell me, these people, the few, the select who make it to heaven don't have to live a sin-free life? They don't have to be perfect after accepting God and Jesus as their Savior?" I ask skeptically.

"No. That's the crazy part. It appears it all has to do with surrender. Once a person really believes in God, once they really believe that Jesus died on the cross for their sins, once they really believe...I mean no more doubt; I mean, they pray to God when no one is around, we are talking about not only praying but expecting results, you know, they really believe He is there. We're not just talking about public prayer. No more 'look at me'. We are talking in the corner in the dark where no one else can hear or see. Another one of God's tests. If you don't really believe there is a God and that you have access to Him, you are not going to spend any time on your knees praying to something that you don't believe is there. At least something you believe is listening. So once again God has played this little joke on all the brilliant people. You see, only the people who genuinely believe spend time in prayer. The pretenders only pray when they feel others expect it of them."

"I'm drowning. What you are saying? You can't earn your way into heaven?"

"Right. Let's look at Colossians 2:11, where it says,

> *You were dead in sin, and your sinful desires were not yet cut away. Then He gave you a share in the life of Christ, for He forgave all of your sins, and blotted out the charges proved against you, the list of His commandments which you had not obeyed. He took this list of sins and destroyed it by nailing it to Christ's cross. In this way God took away Satan's power to accuse you of sin, and God openly displayed to the whole world Christ's triumph at the cross where your sins were all taken away.*

"The only way you can get to heaven is if you truly believe Jesus is the Son of God and he died on the cross for your sins?" I wonder.

"Yes," says the Eluder.

"But it's so simple."

"Yeah, but only a few get it. The one thing I can promise you is, we will always have lots of company down here, Pervert. People want their own way. We are all very selfish. When given a choice, we will almost always take the easy route. We don't want to suffer. We want it now. We want the best car, the best house, the best food, the best sex, the best job. We want to be first. We look at second place as a losing position, as undesirable. Who did you know with the philosophy of God first and others second?"

"No one."

"I rest my case."

"Oh, wait a minute, Mother Theresa!"

"Well, no chance you are going to run into Mother Theresa down here. As I recall, one of the Dark Angels was telling us that when she died, he was near the great chasm, and he said you could see rainbows and stars everywhere and the Holy Choir sang so loud that they could be heard on our side."

"What is the great chasm?"

"It is where you can see the very edge of the Kingdom. You can even speak to someone from the other side. They usually don't stay in that area very long. I think that is where they go when they first arrive. They have something like orientation and move on."

"How do you get there?"

"It's close to where the people in your vision are. Only Dark Angels can pass through on our side without great pain. Everyone else enters there to be processed. Once processed, you are then moved to the area where our lord assigns you.

"So even if you could reach the great chasm, you still couldn't cross it?"

"No. In fact, there was a case in the manual referring to the great chasm. Let's see, where is that? Oh yeah, here it is."

> Luke 16:19: "*There was a certain rich man." Jesus said, "who was splendidly clothed and lived each day in mirth and luxury. One day Lazarus, a diseased beggar, was laid at his door. As he lay there longing for scraps from the rich man's table, the dogs would come and lick his open sores. Finally the beggar died and was carried by the angels to be with Abraham in the place of the righteous dead. The rich man died and was also buried, and his soul went into hell. There, in torment, he saw Lazarus in the far distance with Abraham.*
>
> *"'Father Abraham.' he shouted, 'have some pity! Send Lazarus over here if only to dip the tip of his finger in water and cool my tongue, for I am in anguish in these flames."*
>
> *But Abraham said to him, 'Son, remember that during your lifetime you had everything you wanted, and Lazarus had nothing. So now he is here being comforted and you are in anguish. And besides, there is a great chasm separating us, and anyone wanting to come to you from here is stopped at its edge: and no one over there can cross to us.'*
>
> *"Then the rich man said, 'O Father Abraham, then please send him to my father's home—for I have five brothers—to warn them about this place of torment lest they come here when they die.'*
>
> *"But Abraham said. 'The Scriptures have warned them again and again. Your brothers can read them any time they want to.'*
>
> *"The rich man replied. 'No, Father Abraham, they won't bother to*

read them. But if someone is sent to them from the dead, then they will turn from their sins.'

"But Abraham said. 'If they won't listen to Moses and the prophets, they won't listen even though someone rises from the dead.'"

"So, as you can see, the great Abraham, 'Father of the Jews,' said there is no way to pass through the great chasm."

"I tell you, I am innocent! I didn't know what I was doing."

"Let's see what the ol' manual says. Ah, this is it."

Romans 1:18–21 *But God shows his anger from heaven against all sinful, evil men who push away the truth from them. For the truth about God is known to them instinctively: God has put this knowledge in their hearts. Since earliest times men have seen the earth and sky and all God made, and have known of his existence and the great eternal power. So they will have no excuse [when they stand before God at Judgment Day]. Yes, they knew about him all right, but they wouldn't admit it or worship him or even thank him for all his daily care. And after a while they began to think up silly ideas of what God was like and what he wanted them to do. The result was that their foolish minds became dark and confused. Claiming themselves to be wise without God, they became utter fools instead.*

"Did you get that, Pervert?"

"What about these preachers I've heard at funerals say things about someone who didn't attend church and wasn't walking with Jesus, like, 'Bob has gone on to meet his maker and have eternal peace.' What kind of lie was that?"

"Poor little boy. You didn't read the manual, so you couldn't identify the goats and the sheep. You didn't know that some men are preachers because the road to being a pastor is easier than the one where they have to get out there and bust their hump. Let's see, how will Jesus receive your petition? He will probably refer you to the following:"

Matthew 7:15–20: *Beware of false teachers who come disguised as harmless sheep, but are wolves and will tear you apart. You can detect them by the way they act, just as you can identify a tree by its fruit. You need never confuse grapevines with thorn bushes or figs with thistles. Different kinds of fruit trees can quickly be identified by examining their fruit a variety that produces delicious fruit never produces an inedible kind. And a tree producing an inedible kind can't produce what is good. So the trees having the inedible fruit are chopped down and thrown on the fire. Yes, the way to identify a tree or a person is by the kind of fruit produced.*

"So I guess it would be nice if God would give you that out. Then you could say, 'But, Lord, I was taught wrong.' People who go before Him with such a weak defense won't even get a glance. He will say to you, 'Who cares what the preacher said? Was it consistent with my word?' And you will say?"

"I didn't read the book!"

"Did you read that *Playboy* you subscribed to for eight years? How about that *Hustler?* Did you read those manuals at your office so you would know more than the others? Did you read those four Stephen King novels?"

"Stop!....Yes."

"Bad choices. You chose to read all that garbage. All that time reading something that gave you instant gratification. Yet you read nothing that would save your eternal soul. Nothing that would keep you out of here. You know, Pervert, to say you are a man who made bad decisions just doesn't get it. Let's tell it like it is. You're an idiot!" His laugh is angry.

'Well, I guess you weren't on the Dean's list either."

The Eluder is grabbing me by the throat with one hand.

"I'm not the one whining, Pervert. I did the crime, I'm doing the time. The time is life without parole, Sissy."

He releases his death grip.

"Man, I can't get my breath, I'm weak as water. How many times are you going to kill me?"

"Again and again until I get it right."

"I guess we won't talk about your shortcomings?"

The Eluder groans.

"Okay, what about the Faiths? I hung out with this gal who was from a different background and, man, they have a different look. She said they don't read the Bible. The priest interprets it for them. So most of them don't read the Bible. What about them?"

"What did I just read you about the false prophets, idiot?"

"You mean even the religious groups who thought they were doing the right thing by listening to their leaders are going to find themselves in hell?"

"The fruit trees, Pervert, the fruit trees. What kind of fruit are they producing? If you have never read the book, it's kinda hard to obey what it says. How could you get answers to your everyday questions? I mean, if the book is the manual of life and you have a question about life, who do you call? Ghostbusters? A little humor, idiot. Duh...I guess you would read the manual. Then if you were walking with Jesus, you would check with Him for clarification."

"How would you check with God for clarification?" I laugh.

"Prayer, Pervert. According to God, He wants to have a personal relationship with His children. Well, how do you have a personal relationship with someone? Come on, you can do this. Okay, you talk to them, and they talk to you. So when you read the book, God is talking to you, and when you pray, you are talking to God. Now, according to common sense, this is now a personal relationship. So when they pray to their Father, they ask Him for help in different things. Then, as they read the Bible, they learn who their Father and their Lord are, so they can understand how to please them."

"You know, the problem I have with this whole thing is that it seems as though God just wants people to be His servants. Well, I'm nobody's servant."

"Boy, are you an idiot! You are Satan's servant."

"I never chose Satan as my lord."

"Yes, you did, Pervert."

"No, I didn't. I have no lord because I chose no master."

"Well, there's where you don't get it. But you're not alone. Half, if not more, of planet earth doesn't get it either. So I'll try and not make fun of you at this point. You see, Pervert, there are only two choices. There is Good and Evil, righteousness and self- serving, serving God or Satan. I guess people don't like those two choices. So they try to create a third choice. It can be political correctness, achievement, walking to one's own beat. Doesn't matter. They all are serving number two. You see, to serve anything other than God is to serve Satan. See why we do so well down here? That's why the road to hell is wide. Any choice other than following God leads here, idiot. That's why the road to heaven is narrow and only a few get in. Now, why would the word of God say that? The very definition of God is Truth. Yet all these idiots think they know what is right and what is wrong. Now, if God said the road is narrow and only a few get in, then guess what? All these people who are saying, 'My God is a loving, forgiving God,' are full of it.

"God can't lie. Think about it. Whatever He says is so, because whatever He says comes to pass as He speaks it. So explain how people got so high and mighty that they could actually change the meaning of God's word. Wow! What brilliant people! Though God said, 'It's my way or the highway,' these great people have decided that God was politically incorrect and 'they' have corrected Him. Now, they have perverted—no offense—His word, so it's okay to take an unborn life if it puts the mother out. It's okay to be gay. Why, they have even started homosexual churches. So what does God know? I guess, even though He is great enough to create the earth, He wasn't as smart as the politically correct. So His ideas are outdated. God created man, but He didn't give any thought to the future. So now men have recreated God in their image. Only one problem, Pervert—God's word is not open for debate. Gee, what a bummer. All the politicians will be broken-hearted. All those captains of the debate teams will be so sad.

"Here is the problem as I see it, Pervert. God created man. He asked for acknowledgment. All man can do for God is honor him. The only way man can honor Him is to acknowledge he exists. The only way man can truly acknowledge God's existence is through having a personal relationship with him. Ah, there is that catch-22. The only way to have a personal relationship with Him, as we discussed before, to pray—talk to God—and to read His word—listen to God. To be a child of the living God is to be obedient to Him.

"Oh, no! There's the problem! God expects man to obey Him, not question Him, not ignore Him, not to put words in His mouth, not rebel against Him. So what do you think all these politically correct people are going to do? I mean, they had their own way on earth, just as you and I. Now it's time to pay the ticket. Step up to the box. The question is, did you obey? Wait, wait, wait. The question is, did you obey? Did you submit to God, or did you want your own way? If you chose your own way, then your ticket is punched, and it reads, 'Down."

I break in. "That's it? You mean there is no gray area? It's that black and white? You either worship God while on the earth or burn in hell for eternity? Any intelligent man knows there are several philosophies on God's willingness to forgive."

"Correct. But God has no gray area. You are one of the saved or one of the unsaved. There is no limbo. Ah…here is what God thinks of your intellectual ability. Listen."

> 1 Corinthians 20–25: *So what about these wise men, these scholars, these brilliant debaters of this worlds great affairs? God has made them all look foolish, and shown their wisdom to be useless nonsense. For God in his wisdom saw to it that the world would never find God through human brilliance, and then he stepped in and saved all those who believed his message, which the world calls foolish and silly. It seems foolish to the Jews because they want a sign from heaven as proof that what is preached is true; and it is foolish to the gentiles because they believe only what agrees with their philosophy and seems wise to them. So when it is preached about Christ dying to save them, the Jews are offended and the gentiles say it's all nonsense. But God has opened the eyes of those called to salvation, both Jews and Gentiles, to see that Christ is the mighty power of God to save them; Christ himself is the center of God's wise plan for their salvation. This so-called "foolish" plan of God is far wiser than the wisest plan of the wisest man, and God in his weakness (Christ dying on the cross) is far Stronger than any man.*

"Okay, Jerry's up."

Jerry says, "Honey, I'm going to get up for a while and study."

"Sweetheart, you work so hard. I don't see how you have the energy to get your Master's. I'm exhausted when I get home. How do you do it?"

"I want us to have a good life, babe. Rest a little while longer, and I'll get you up in time for your bath."

"I love you, sweetie," Amy purrs.

Jerry responds, "You too."

The Eluder exhorts, "Hey, Jerry, you've been busting your butt. Why not take a little time off?"

The Ghost interrupts, "Of course, if you want that degree, you better keep your nose to the grindstone."

"Hey, that movie you were talking about is coming on tonight," notifies the Eluder.

The Ghost smiles as He says, "There's plenty of time for that."

"Hey, Jerry, isn't there a cheat sheet on the Internet? You could get the test and the answers in ten minutes. Hey, let's go for it," tempts the Eluder.

The Ghost augments, "Yeah, but you want the knowledge. Knowledge is power, right, Jerry?"

Amy calls, "Honey, that crazy Julie is on the phone, and she swears this is the last time she is going to ask us to go to church. There is this special service with some preacher who is one of the top pastors in the country. He is speaking at their church. What do you say? It might be interesting."

"Does Julie promise this is the last time she will ask us?"

"Hold on....Yes, this is positively the last time," Amy snickers.

"Good, then this is the last time I have to say...no!"

"Jerry's being ugly. Hope you have a great time. Okay, okay. I love you, too."

"So what did she say?" questions Jerry.

"She said she will keep her promise. She really sounded sad."

"Take her to Ben and Jerry's and she'll get over it," Jerry snickers.

"Honey, do you really think going to church is a sellout?"

"Yeah. I'm not going to attend a church when I'm not sincere. To me that's a lie."

The Eluder validates, "That's right, Jerry. The churches are loaded with hypocrites. At least Amy will never doubt your honor. I mean, look at Julie—she gives you that little come-on look and then she goes in to the church like the rest of them and acts like she is some sort of saint. None of that here."

Suddenly there is the roar of a freight train combined with thunder, and we are overlooking an area with thousands of orbs.

"What is that?"

The Governor CHIRZPA, he who enjoys loud sounds, just passed.

"What's going on? Where are we?"

"We aren't needed in that battle anymore," offers the Eluder.

"What does that mean? Did we lose?"

"*Au contraire*. We were winning by such a great margin, there was no need to continue."

"How can that be? Jerry was a straight arrow. He rejected everything you threw at him. How is it we left ahead?"

"Did you hear Jerry tell his wife he has no use for the church?"

"Yes."

"Man! Don't you get it? The only thing we are doing is recruiting. If the person isn't interested in God and the church, then guess who gets him, Pervert."

"You mean even though Jerry is a straight arrow, honest as the day is long, faithful to his wife, he is going to hell?"

"Yes."

"How can that be? What kind of God would send Jerry to hell?"

"The God that created Jerry and loved him and created him for His own purpose. The only reason Jerry exists is to serve God. Jerry was given life, but he was also given the freedom to make his own choices. If you think about it, it makes perfect sense. Why would God create all these people and have them run around like little robots? They would all fall down on their faces and praise God at noon and again at 5:00 P.M. I mean, even you would get tired of that. God, on the other hand, has wisdom; therefore He knew that wouldn't be satisfying. He also knew if He soared through the earth and was visible to man, it would be a case where people would fear Him, not adore Him, not really love Him, just be afraid of Him. So in all his wisdom He creates man and allowed early man to feel His presence, allowed prophets to record His word, had Jesus walk the earth in the non-threatening body of a man. This was so everyone who wanted to believe in God could have the proof they needed. There is historical evidence that Jesus walked the earth, and He was the only one to lead a perfect life. He fulfilled over 300 prophecies. Do you know what the odds are that someone could fulfill over 300 prophecies that took place over 1000 years? Impossible. Can't happen. Yet Jesus did it.

"Well," continues the Eluder, "anyone who really wants to believe now has the information to prove that God and Jesus really exist. The true beauty of God's plan is that only the people with a soft, loving heart can find Him. You have to rely on faith alone. God isn't hovering in the sky for all to see. Jesus isn't here as a man anymore. As I read to you earlier, God made all of us with the knowledge that He is real, but the pressure of society made many push back the truth. Deep inside we know the truth. The risk of ridicule is real and great. Nobody wants to be laughed at; nobody wants to be separated out. So only those with real courage are able to continue on a course that allows them to walk with God. Think about it—God made it so only the true gladiators would be with Him. You see, not that many have the courage to stand up to the rest of the world and say 'Jesus is Lord of my life'. Oh, yeah, I know all the evangelists stand up and claim Jesus, but I'm talking about true gladiators. The ones who have nothing to gain financially. The ones that only stand to be ridiculed, and yet they are acknowledging God every day.

"Well, Pervert, that's who you will find in heaven. Do you understand how many people that leaves out of your equation?

"Okay, hold on, a Dark Angel is passing," alerts the Eluder.

"Man, he's scary," I whisper. "Look at all those orbs! How can there be so much light in this place? This looks like a science fiction movie. What are those…those, for lack of a better word, electrical currents doing running from one orb to another?"

"That is the force field that alerts the Holy Ghost. The place you are looking at, though it looks like it is right in front of you, is a long ways from us. We are observing only as a privilege because we were ahead in the last battle before being brought here.

"The energy field and the brilliant light is coming from you know who. The great energy surging through the area and connecting to each of the orbs is a great monitor. This is controlled by the High Priest Melchizedek."

"Who is Melchizedek?"

The Eluder says, "Well, where is it? Okay. Listen to this:"

> Hebrews 5:6: *That is why Christ did not elect himself to the honor of being High Priest: no, he was chosen by God. God said to him, "My Son, today I have honored you." And another time God said to him, "You have been chosen to be a priest forever, with the same rank as Melchizedek.*

"Notice the Scripture didn't say a position *over* Melchizedek. That should give you some idea of how powerful he is. History says there is no record of Melchizedek's birth or his death. Melchizedek is the High Priest. He governs the monitoring of the orbs. The orbs are monitored to see if anyone has a change of heart."

"What do you mean, 'a change of heart'?" I interjected.

"Okay. For example, someone calls out to God. Someone who is not a Christian. Someone says, 'If there is really a God, hear me'. In other words, someone tries to make contact with God. Even though he doesn't know how to make contact with God, the orb starts illuminating and pulsating and a weird noise starts to come from it. The noise is hearsay, because you have to be close to the orb to hear the weird noise. The only reason I know this is I overheard a Dark Angel talking about it. He said it was unlike anything he had ever heard.

"Once these things start to happen, the monitor administrators assign an Angel of Light, or the Ghost, as we call him, as well as an Angel of Darkness. They originate the battle. Once the battle is underway, the Dark Angel will assign an Eluder to take over."

"Then what? What happens if the Angel of Light wins?"

"Then the person in the orb goes to the next level."

"What level is that?"

"He receives the Spirit man, and we never see him again."

"Why?"

"I'm not sure. I was told that once a person has the Spirit man, only the Dark Angels can enter the orb with him."

"So what's the difference?"

"Are you kidding? Once a person has the Holy Spirit in him, he wants to please God. It's not like a worldly person who is trying to please himself. These people are reading the Bible, going to church, and praying. They have so much more information, it is difficult to get them to turn away.

"When the person in the orb gets upset with us, it's just too bad, but when someone with the Spirit man gets upset with a Dark Angel, they can cast them out. Satan has made this process very painful for the Dark Angels. When they are thrown from the orb, Satan has a torture chamber right outside awaiting them."

"How do they have the power to throw the Dark Angels out?"

"When they receive the Holy Spirit, they have the power of God in them. They have a direct line of communication with God himself. They have so much power that Jesus once said that anyone with this power, with the proper faith, could say to a mountain 'move' and it would move. Here we go:"

> Mark 11:22–23 *In reply Jesus said to the disciples, "If you only have faith in God—this is the absolute truth—you can say to this Mount of Olives, 'Rise up and fall into the Mediterranean," and your command will be obeyed. All that's required is that you really believe and have no doubt!"*

"So the person who is a child of God can cry out to God, and head 'em up, move 'em out. That's what we call a bad day around here. The good news is these children of God seem to try everything in their power to solve their own problems before they turn to God. That part is great. This gives us the chance to inflict a lot of pain. In some cases we actually win them over because they didn't ask God to intervene."

"Why would someone with that kind of power choose not to use it?"

"Well, you got me, Pervert. I don't have a clue. They just struggle and grovel along. All the time God is right there. Go figure."

"Maybe it's pride?"

"I guess. You gotta have a lot of pride to ignore God. If I were a child of God, my slogan would be 'Don't leave home without Him'."

"Yeah, me too. Let's kick some butt. If I can't go to heaven, then I'll bring as many as possible down here with me."

"Well, I think you're getting it now, Pervert."

"Okay, tell me more about what I'm going to face. Are most of them Christians or people like Jerry?"

"Most are Christians.

"There are thirty Aries that service most of the world. For example, DEO is the Aethyr of selfishness. MAZ is Aethyr of appearance. BAG is Aethyr of doubt. ICH is Aethyr of tension, and so on. They justify all the feelings the world has, anything that might keep one from going to God. There are thirty basic sectors of the thought process that can lead man away from God. These are the areas the Aries cover. As long as a child of the world is content in one of these sectors, they don't require a lot of maintenance."

"Explain what you mean by 'sectors'."

"Okay, let's say a child of the world is into traveling. NIA, Aethyr of traveling, is assigned to that person. NIA will continue to encourage that person to put their self-worth in travel."

"I don't get it. What do you mean, 'self-worth in travel'?"

"Some people like to travel because it makes them feel important. So even if the job means losing their spouse, costing them friendships, etc., they are willing to do whatever it takes to continue to travel. They live for the opportunity to enter a room and have someone say 'Oh, where have you been this time?'"

"Could that be a traveling salesman?"

"Yes. Many times the traveling salesman doesn't make enough to justify the job. But those benefits are hard to give up. Nights in motels away from the responsibilities of a family. Hey, they can go out and party like a single person, yet have the status of the married. In some cases NIA even allows them to be martyred by their family. Poor Dad has to travel so much he misses all the wonderful things a father lives for. Yeah, like changing diapers. Going to soccer games in the rain or freezing cold. Putting up with the kid's fights. Poor baby."

"Give me another Aethyr."

"LIL, the first Aethyr, controls a sector of humans who have an insatiable desire to be first in anything they do. It's that human who has to get in front of you at the next light. You would think they must be late for an appointment. Not so. LIL feeds this desire. As long as they are preoccupied with being first, they can't be serving anyone. This is great because a lot of these humans would be great children of God, but they are too fixed on this first thing. Usually these people draw people to them until others see this 'first' thing. Then they back away slowly and in most cases undetected. This is to our advantage, because it makes it difficult for them to see the affects of their actions.

"Another is ARN, Aethyr of fulfillment. This is a great one. The 'modern man' has helped us so much. Everything you see is about self-fulfillment. You know, Pervert, the key is as long as you can keep someone thinking about himself, you are doing a great job of recruiting. The worst candidate is someone who is always thinking about someone else. We love it when we hear 'I need fulfillment'. ARN put a hidden meaning in the word 'fulfillment'. We decode it like this: full-fill me'-nt. It is all about fill me. I want to fill my cup. Guess what? The upside is you can fill that cup, for the most, about sixty years if you're lucky. Imagine, to fill one's self for sixty years on that miserable planet, you would be willing to spend eternity in hell." The Eluder laughs. "Boy, and these people think they are being good to themselves. Bad choices, Pervert. Bad choices."

"While we are waiting, give me another one."

"Why?"

"Because it makes me feel better when I realize I'm not the only idiot."

"The third Aethyr is ZOM, the Aethyr of self-knowledge. It is said that ZOM entertains God. ZOM feeds the arrogance of man. Modern man has made a mistake. They have told their children, 'You are so smart'. They tell them, 'You can do anything'," the Eluder bellows.

"What's wrong with that?"

"That is exactly what we want them to tell them. Now, little Johnny grows up and thinks of himself as some divine being. Little Johnny can do anything he sets his mind to do. Big problem, Pervert. Who does Johnny need? Does little Johnny say God first, others second? No. Little Johnny is ours. His parents, who thought they were creating self-confidence, created a little monster. They created someone who thinks too highly of himself and doesn't need others. The thing God hates most is pride and haughtiness."

> Proverbs 19: *For there are six things the Lord hates —no, seven:*
> *Haughtiness*
> *Lying*
> *Murdering*
> *Plotting evil*
> *Eagerness to do wrong*
> *A false witness*
> *Sowing discord among brothers*

"What is important is twofold. What did he say the Lord feels about these things? He said the Lord hates these things. There are many superlatives he could have used to describe the way the Lord feels about these things, but he used the word HATE. Not dislikes or frowns upon, but hates. Second, which did he list first? Haughtiness. When it comes to the manual, everything is relevant. God's number one on his hate list is pride and haughtiness. You asked earlier what the problem was with teaching your child to think highly of himself or herself? Well, now little Johnny thinks the world revolves around him. What wonderful thing should he undertake now? You see, Johnny has all this potential, now he has to use it. This means he is running wide open trying to achieve, trying to prove Mommy and Daddy right. When the agenda is proving you are capable and productive, there is no room for others. These people have a hard enough time

keeping a spouse, let alone giving themselves to someone in need. This is why a little known verse in the Bible reads, *Flattery is a form of hatred and wounds cruelly' (Proverbs 26:28).* Those who are aware of this verse still don't get it. They think it's just one of those verses that doesn't really apply. They all apply! Does this help you understand why excessive praising of children is a big mistake?"

"Wow, I really can't believe it. All those people! Thinking they are doing the right thing. Telling their kids how wonderful they are," I marvel.

"Have you ever heard, 'The road to hell is paved with good intentions'?"

"Yeah, but I never paid that much attention to it."

"Hey, look at it this way. We are going to have lots of company," the Eluder snickers.

"Man, give me another one."

"Okay, PAZ, Aethyr of impending expression."

"Impending expression? What the hell is that?"

"He promotes and encourages people who don't quite say what it is they really want. They hint around, but never express their true feelings."

"I hate those kind of people."

"PAZ reinforces their feelings of self-righteousness. He reassures them that the problem is the other person. These humans love to feel righteous indignation. So to allow themselves the ability to feel righteous, they have to spin a web that can get complicated. They give information, but never enough that someone can hold their feet to the fire…yet!"

"Got it."

"So, this way, they can give you a little information, and if you prove them wrong, they didn't give you enough to really slam them, so they carefully change their position, then merely explain you misunderstood what they were saying—'You figure it out'. This way they can't be cornered. To be wrong is too great a price for them to pay. So these kind of people spend their whole lives being dishonest just to avoid being wrong. What egos! What a waste of time and energy! These are also the type that when you point out something to them, and it's irrefutable, the next time you are around them, they are quoting what you said verbatim. Yet they will never acknowledge that the information came from you. Being right is just too important. When being right is everything, and you're willing to burn whoever it takes to avoid being wrong, you are going to make some bad choices."

"Who else?"

"LIT is an Aethyr without a supreme being. He keeps affirming that there is no God. There is only what you see.

"So he was a Darwin kind a guy? I guess Darwin was really surprised to find out he was wrong?"

"Yeah—the only problem is he found out before he died."

"What?"

"That's what I said. He gave all his money to the church. He died a Christian. What a hoot! Think about it. All these idiots who quote Darwin and have those fish that read inside 'Darwin' instead of 'Jesus' on their bumper are so stupid. They didn't do any follow-up. They just read his book or attended a class on evolution and accepted it. There has never been one species to evolve from one species to another during man's existence on this planet. Yet these humans believe this is how man began. The 'Big Bang' theory has absolutely nothing to back it up. Those losers want to believe in anything but God so bad, they'll accept anything. It's our job to help them out. So what if there's really nothing to prove the Big Bang or Darwin's theory on evolution? That isn't important. You see, these people who want an answer are willing to accept almost anything to escape God. They don't want to be held accountable. See, if I don't believe there is a God, then I don't have to follow him. If I don't have to follow him, then I am free to do whatever I feel like, oh yeah. and not feel guilty. LIT is one of our lord's favorite Aries because he nurtures their unpardonable sin."

"You mean they can't be forgiven of their sin?"

"Right. This is the only sin that is not forgiven by the blood of Jesus: to blaspheme the Holy Spirit. In other words, to say God does not exist. Remember when I read to you that God put in every man's heart knowledge of God's existence? So when a man chooses to block that out and denies God exists, then this is the sin that will not go unpunished."

"Okay. Give me one more."

'MAZ, the Aethyr of appearances. MAZ has a difficult time. He must keep these people distracted. They are almost always people with low self-esteem. These people don't usually stay in this condition. Success at work. A loving spouse. An adoring child. All of these things can change a person who has an appearance addiction. These are usually people who need that little extra confidence to get through the day. The beauty is, if you can keep them in this cycle, it can be self-destructive. MAZ informed us that these people are often the major contributors to credit card debt. A good clotheshorse can spend what he or she makes on clothes alone. This within itself isn't all that bad. But what it causes is a beautiful thing: debt. That's right. The number one cause for divorce. Boy, there's no better example of cause and effect than a clotheshorse. MAZ has some of these people so hooked that they drive junkers and live in a dive just so they can get all dressed up." The Eluder howls, "What idiots. Appearance is everything, baby," he cackles. "All dressed up and nowhere to go. They go to all the 'in' functions and stand around like they are going to be discovered or something. When you go back home, you're back in the old neighborhood and you say to yourself, 'No one I went to school with is still out there. They're all settled down.' No, these people are still out there waiting to be discovered," he howls. "Bad choices."

"Okay, okay, you were standing on my toes. Give me another one."

"DEO, the Aethyr of selfishness. He must continually feed these humans. They are very active. Mixed properly, greed and selfishness grow like weeds. As selfishness and greed are brothers, they come from the same house. Greed is truly one of our best sins! The more you get, the more you want. Can't beat that. DEO gave a seminar on how it works. He gave a formula that I can't remember, but it went something like this: As someone reaches for something either emotionally or physically, a reactionary table is put in motion. The example looked like an orb with a protractor around it. Sometimes there was only one person in the orb-looking thing, and sometimes there were more. It was really exciting to watch it work. Every time the person started drawing the object or circumstance toward himself, you could see with the help of the gauge on the object the effect it had on the other people. As the person drew the object or circumstance closer to himself, you could see by the scale as to how important it was to each of the other people and as to how far they were pushed back from the person drawing it to themselves. Hard to explain, but a great example. Oh, well, you had to be there."

'What do you mean when he pulled it toward him, they moved away?"

"Yes, something like that. Each time the person reached out for something, he activated the device. The sliding scales would light up, and the positions of the other people would be shown like the latitude and longitude of a spot on the map. As DEO explained, some of the people were closer to this person than others. The reason varied. It had to do with two things—how much they cared for the person and how important the object or occurrence was to them. A few were very close, and others were scattered in different locations. It always depended on how many people were aware of what was happening.

"As the person would reach out for an object, all eyes were on him. As he would draw it closer to himself, the people would start disconnecting. First, at the exact rate the object was moving toward him, they would move away from him. Then at different points, depending on how much this person meant to them, they would just disconnect. Some of them worked with him, and some were family. The ones who worked with him disconnected much faster. The strange thing is the friends took a lot longer to disconnect, but once they did, they permanently disassociated. The first to disconnect and the last to leave were family."

"You know, my father was always taking the best of everything. I thought he just didn't like me."

"Hey, you're not the lone ranger. Almost everybody who is connected with a selfish person feels rejection and they take it personally. This is our strong point. The selfish person is injuring everyone around him or her. Now, we have all these hurt people. They're just looking for something to attach themselves to. So what is our best tool? It's television! That's right, boys and girls. Mommy and Daddy don't give a hoot about you. They are too self-centered. So just sit back and let the entertainment world show you right from wrong." He roars, "What a blast! Little Johnny is watching Jerry Springer to find out what direction to take. What a trip! Old Jerry will show little Johnny how to reach us. If we could just get old Jerry to put our phone number on at the end of the show, he could help speed the process along. When you are young and your parents are selfish, when they are more interested in being your friend than being your parent, you are in deep trouble."

"I wish my father had been my friend."

"You just think you do. A wise man would wish his father would accept the responsibilities of being a real father. That ain't your friend, Pervert. A real father would never let a young child sit alone in front of a TV without supervision. I don't care how unpopular he becomes. A good father would make sure each child in his home knew the Bible and had a personal relationship with Jesus. Then he could die knowing his children were assured eternal life somewhere other than here."

"On second thought, I vote for the same father."

"Everybody wants to be liked. But the price of being your children's best friend is too great. 'Mommy, Mommy, can we just watch this one show? It only has a few bad words in it, and we won't listen.' Hey, Mommy was made to love and nurture. She wants her children to enjoy what everybody else enjoys. So what kind of dad do they have? One who would rather be the good guy. One where all the children say, 'Thanks, Dad, you're the greatest.' It takes a strong man to say no and be the bad guy. The thing is, more and more dads are crumbling because they sent their wives out of the home into the workplace. Now they feel guilty. So what do you do to coat yourself in feel good stuff? Let everybody do what they want and you're a hero, but only for a while, sucker.

"A father is the head of the home. God doesn't care that the politically correct beg to differ. When the head of the home drops the ball, it's almost impossible to make the adjustments necessary to save the children. The father's job is to teach the children discipline and to draw the lines so they will know where their limits are. Then, when they are grown, they will feel safe because they know what is right and what is wrong. That is in contrast with the father who says the sky is the limit. You can do anything. The child knows nothing of what is expected of him. He knows no right from wrong. He lives with the frustration of unrealistic goals and never feeling safe and secure within himself. This gives us the perfect opportunity to do our thing. His self-image is distorted, making him the ideal victim. Ain't life grand?"

"Are you saying a person shouldn't tell a child they can do anything they want if they put forth the effort?" I inquire.

"Right, because that is a lie. They can't do anything they can imagine. That simply isn't true. Everyone has limitations. Everyone has gifts. The key to balance is to know who you are. This doesn't mean you can't excel at something. If you pay attention to some athletes, you notice they are pointing that finger up to God. They acknowledge God, while attempting to maximize their achievement with the abilities God gave them and always remembering who gave them the gift. Putting God first gives them a great advantage in life. Even when they have immense success, they keep things in a proper perspective. They understand it's not all about them.

"So," the Eluder continues, "Father tells child, 'You can do anything you want. You can be anybody you want to be.' Child hits high school and finds out that isn't true. There are kids better at almost everything than he or she is. Now what? A child that has a distorted self-image can't cope with the reality. You want to know why some kids in today's world go nuts and start shooting up the school? It's because they're ticked. Their mommy and daddy told them the sky was the limit. Hey, what sky? Most of the kids at school can outperform them at anything they try. They aren't popular. The warm and cuddly things Mom and Dad told them about their selves were not confirmed at school. So, now what? Where do these kids go? Mom and Dad said if I gave it my all, I could do anything. Either my parents are liars or I'm substandard. Poor kid, they must guard this secret from everybody. If they tell the kids at school there has been a mistake, they were slated to be one of the chosen, they'll be laughed out of the school. They can't tell their parents because the ugly truth will come out. The truth is they feel a disappointment to their parents, so they must keep this secret bottled up inside. You see, it's not okay to be average anymore. Second place is a losing position. Great, uh?"

"Who would have ever thought telling your child they are special would be harmful to them?" I offer.

'To say they are special is not distorting the truth. They are special to their parents, and they are special to God."

"Then where do the parents go wrong?"

"They don't teach them humility. They paint a picture for their child that gives the child the impression they are special to everyone. Haven't you seen a child misbehaving and everyone around was put out?"

"Yes."

"Think about it. The parents didn't correct the child; they just tried to reason with him. Now you've got the tail wagging the dog. Here is little Johnny at three years old controlling all these adults. Why? The parents think they are doing the child a service. Some of the modern-day quacks tell them this is the way to raise your child—to reason with him. How can the child learn where the boundaries are? If the child doesn't agree with the parent, then what? The circus goes on and on. The parents want the child to be something other than a child. That makes the parents something other than parents. Some things stay the same. If it ain't broke, don't fix it. If Daddy wants a best friend, get a dog. Daddy has to be the disciplinarian for the family to function properly. You can't be a child's best friend and their parent, too. The job description reads parent."

"Thank God I didn't have any children. Who's next?"

"ZID is Aethyr of one's god."

"Excuse me, that doesn't even make sense."

"ZID encourages people to decide for themselves who their god is. You don't know much about Christianity, so let me explain. A lot of people want to do the right thing. They can't live up to what their parents told them was true. They don't want to be politically correct. They want to be in the group going to heaven. They basically feel like there is a heaven, but they're not 100 percent sure. So they attend church. They put their children in Sunday school classes so no one can say their children were deprived. Now, this doesn't mean that they are going to fall down on their knees when they are alone. They're not going to read the Bible every night.

"Once, ZID spoke about these people, and he said they use words like, 'Don't get carried away,' 'Let's not go to extremes,' 'They sound like fanatics.' ZID stated that these people have their own idea of what God should be, based on how they perceive right and wrong. It has nothing to do with God's word. Go figure. Who can understand that? Well, the beauty is we don't have to understand. All we have to do is stand at the door and let them in. Ha ha! ZID said you can tell one of his children when they say, 'My God wouldn't...'. That's a real hoot. They are walking contradictions. They say they are Christians, and yet they will tell you they don't believe the Bible is God's word. These people must be great shoppers. They just take what they want. If it's something they don't like, they just leave it. Well, that works great when shopping, but that won't work when it comes to God's word."

"Boy, what idiots!"

'To the contrary. Most of these people are better educated than the general masses. In most cases ZJD said they were products of parents who told them they could do anything or they could be anybody. So their world is distorted. They don't see their limits. Their father never set boundaries for them. These people, although they mean well, are really far from God. They are not worshiping Him. In their own way they try to acknowledge God, but they lack the proper information. They were never given the gift of a strong conviction; therefore, they make up their perception of God as they go. For example, an active homosexual joins a new circle of friends. They just adopt the viewpoint that their god is a forgiving god and therefore will forgive the homosexual. Listen to this:"

> Romans 1–27: *That is why God let go of them and let them do all these evil things, so that even the women turned against God's natural plan for them and indulged in sex sin with each other. And the men, instead of having a normal sex relationship with a woman, burned with lust for each other, men doing shameful things with other men and, as a result, getting paid within their own souls with the penalty they so richly deserved.*

"Now I ask you, Pervert, does that sound like God is okay with that? Where do they get off with this 'My God is a forgiving God and accepts them, too'. They have confused God's love for God's forgiveness. Hey, get a grip. 'We' are going to love them. They won't need to worry about what God thinks. They'll be so far from Him, it won't make any difference what He thinks." The Eluder smiles.

> Romans 2:4–6: *Don't you realize how patient He is being with you? Or don't you care? Can't you see that He has been waiting all this time without punishing you, to give you time to turn from your sin? His kindness is meant to lead you to repentance. But no, you won't listen: and* .so *you are saving up terrible punishment for yourselves because of your stubbornness in refusing to turn from your sin: for there is going to come a day of wrath when God will be the just Judge of all the world.* 'Romans 2:12–15: *He will punish sin wherever it is found. He will punish the heathen when they sin, even*

though they never had God 's written laws, for down in their hearts they know right from wrong. God's laws are written within them; their own conscience accuses them, or sometimes excuses them. And God will punish the Jews for sinning because they have His written laws but don't obey them. They know what is right but don't do it. The day will surely come when at God's command Jesus Christ will judge the secret lives of everyone, their inmost thoughts and motives: this is all part of God's great plan which I proclaim.

"The problem with this part of God's word is a lot of people who have just been skating around the Bible like to say that the Old Testament is outdated. Well, buckaroos, this is Romans. That means it's in the New Testament, and Paul wrote it. Go figure. Maybe Paul was delusional on that day," he snickers.

"Well, there went the ranch," I lament. "I guess that part of my excuse; the part where I didn't read the Bible won't cut it. I guess as far as God is concerned, I knew in my heart right from wrong. The truth is, I did know the difference between right and wrong. I just wanted my own way. I didn't want someone telling me how to live my life. That included God.

"You know, it also mentioned an excuse. Maybe the fact was that I—like the heathen—didn't really understand the full ramifications of what I was doing. Maybe if I were Jewish and had God's written word, I could be held to a higher standard. However, I'm not Jewish, and therefore, I shouldn't be held to the same level as God's chosen people. The keepers of His word would be expected to know, but certainly that wouldn't apply to someone like me."

"Ah, still planning a jailbreak, Pervert? First, let me explain when Paul was talking about the heathen, he was referring to the people where the Word of God had never reached. You, Pervert, being an American, had the right to choose. So you had the same opportunity your Jewish counterparts did. The difference was the sin. Your sin was complacency, theirs was stubborn self-righteousness. You weren't willing to take either the time or the ridicule required to get the truth. It just wasn't important enough. You were trying so hard to be the center of attention, you just never got off that page."

"Maybe, if there would have been someone in my life to point out the right direction."

"What about your grandmother?"

'She was a sweetheart, but had a few loose screws."

"Why do you say that?"

"Oh, everybody in our family knew Granny was a little too into the Bible and church. She was out there in la-la land."

"You know, you're right, Pervert. She is out there in la-la land because she sure as 'Hell' ain't here," he guffaws. "You really drive me nuts, Pervert. Your grandmother was the salt of the earth. Now, let me get this straight. If only you would have had someone to show you the way? Yet, your grandmother, who was a strong Christian woman, well read in the Bible, and was constantly telling you that you needed to give your life to the Lord, this woman was ridiculed by you and your family?"

"Hey, that's not fair," I protest. "My father, her own son, said she was a fruitcake. He and my sisters were always laughing at her. They would make fun of her when she wasn't around. Why would I listen to her?"

"That's the ticket, wise guy. You knew in your heart that your grandmother was a decent woman, just like in Romans where it said you knew the truth in you heart. You just didn't want to be unpopular with your family, so you joined the gang. You chose the easy way. No ridicule from sisters or dad, and no need to learn the Bible as did your grandmother and, correct me if I'm wrong, but your mother, timid as she was, quietly agreed with your grandmother. And there was the big issue. You just can't be politically correct and be a strong Christian."

What about those preachers who said the Bible was outdated? They said you couldn't take the Bible literally. What about all those churches that backed them up?"

"Okay, let's look at Proverbs 26:6—*To trust a rebel to convey a message is as foolish as cutting of your feet and drinking poison."*

"Wait a minute—these guys were pastors and priests!"

"So what are you saying? Does that mean there are no rebels in the church? You mean God has made the church so holy that we, from here, can't enter? So therefore all men of the religious hierarchy are saintly people?"

"Of course not. I heard about that stuff concerning Jim and Tammy Faye and ole Jimmy Swaggart, or whatever his name was."

"Oh, so you admit there could be some people of high position in the church who are influenced by us?"

"Of course."

"Do you think our lord is stupid?"

"No."

"How would anyone figure any other way to bring the people into hell at a greater rate than tell the sinners they are saved? Think about it, Pervert. If you aren't sinning, then you don't need to change. If God loves you no matter what you do, then why change?

"Look at the simplicity of it. All our lord Satan has to do is lure the people into a false sense of security. Let them think they are okay. It's okay to sell high to one person and low to another. It's okay to play golf on Sunday because you have earned it. It's okay to be a practicing homosexual. It's okay to have sex outside of marriage if you think you might be in love. It's okay to lie to someone to protect your best interests. It's okay to charge on your credit card for things you can't afford. And on and on.

"Hey, it's how you make a living," the Eluder offers. "If you can raise the price and the person isn't the wiser, that means you must be a great salesperson. Of course you're entitled, you have worked hard all week, you have earned the right to play golf. Look at all those lazy dudes who just lay around the house on Sunday; at least you have energy, drive. Boy, what a guy! Wait a minute—if being homosexual was a sin, they wouldn't be starting churches that are for homosexuals, would they? If enough of the perverted community assembles in a building that they call a church and that church will sanctify a pastor, then surely this must be of God. Who would want to marry someone without sleeping with him or her first? How would you know if you were compatible? If you live together for a while, you will know if you are right for each other and won't make a mistake. You know to tell a lie to protect someone is not a sin, it's an act of kindness, even if it's protecting yourself; there is nothing wrong with being kind to yourself. You know, you only live once. Whoever dies with the most toys wins. You can't take it with you, so enjoy it while you can. Look at all those beautiful traps. Does our lord Satan know what he is doing, or what?"

"Do you know how many people you have just included? Man, there isn't anybody left. Everybody falls into one of those categories."

"Really? Which one of those did your grandmother fall in?"

"I don't get it. I remember my mother saying to me once that when she was a kid, everybody in her neighborhood was like my grandmother. Then she said, with a sad expression, 'Only a few are like her now'."

"Isn't that exciting? That's when we know we are taking over a nation. Man, what a rush! The last time we had a victory like this was when we took Israel. Man, that was awesome. Then somehow, when we weren't paying attention—oh, well, no need to dwell on the past. We have learned our lesson. When we take your nation, we will strip it to the point nothing will be left. We won't allow some country to come in and scare these guys. They might panic and turn to the Lord. We must let them get so far from God that they are lost and won't know where to turn. That will be one of our greatest days."

Suddenly there is the most threatening of sounds.

"Oh, man! What was that noise?"

'CHIRZPA. He likes loud sounds, so get used to it."

"Holy sh—what is that?"

It is a man in terrible pain screaming and crying, asking for someone to help him. The being that has him is snarling and smoke is coming from the nostrils. The being has wings and is powerfully built. I have never seen anything that looks so anti-human. The talons from its right hand are actually digging into the flesh of the man screaming. The creature is carrying him like a loaf of bread. This is happening at great speed. Now we've caught the being's eye! Everything seems to be going in slow motion. The creature is looking right through me, as my heart is sinking. There is no mercy in that face.

"That is VSNARDA! The one who casts down into the depths," explains the Eluder.

I notice that the Eluder looks as scared as I am, so I take a chance and ask, "Is that concern I see on your face?"

At first the Eluder says nothing, Then slowly, "He is…the one who comes to get you. If you are of no benefit, he takes you to the place you saw in the vision. If you have been removed and sent to the place of desolation, once you hear OBO IBAH AOZPI cry aloud, you can never return.

"When entering the place of desolation, MOLPAND receives you. MOLPAND removes any joy you may have, any memory of joy, for joy is not permitted. Then you are turned over to ANDISPI, who binds into obedience. ANDISPI imbeds you in a wall or hangs you on permanent hooks or buries you to your waist in the ground of worms or one of the other places he binds his prey. Then comes VIXPALG. To anyone who has half an ear, if your feet are not bound, if ANDISPI left one of your limbs free, then run, crawl, or slither. If you can move, then move with whatever force you have. The horror of what is to come is unthinkable. VIXPALG will come. There will be nowhere to run. MOLPAND will steal your joy; ANDISPI will bind you, for if a man were not bound, he could not stand still for the torture he is about to receive."

I find myself weeping uncontrollably. As I look over at the Eluder, he is weeping also. We don't speak for quite some time. We just weep.

Finally I speak. "What can be done to avoid the place of desolation?"

"It is becoming more difficult to avoid it. They don't need as many Eluders as were once needed. Throughout the world there are more and more countries becoming liberal, having a relaxed attitude about religion. Our lord needs us when the people are potential Christians. Once it has been determined that they are just pretenders, then we don't stay with them. God made the soul. Then he gave man control over his soul. Man chooses his own destiny. If man doesn't call on God, then God leaves him alone. If man pays the least bit of attention to God, He is right there. When man turns his back on God, then God does the same. Well, when man is rocking along, thinking he is doing well, he doesn't need us. God isn't with him, and we don't need to be. You see, he belongs to us. So our master doesn't need us to be there at the orb with them.

"The only problem for us is when a country starts going south, we don't have a lot to do. Therefore our lord needs fewer and fewer Eluders, so it takes less and less to get you eliminated."

"What about all the people who are questioning God? And look at how many more question Jesus. You would think our lord would need lots of Eluders," I interject.

"Do you know how many people die every day? Out of all those people who die, do you know how many come here? And out of the number that come here, do you know how many want to become Eluders versus going to the place you saw in your vision?"

"I guess long-term vacancies are like water coolers down here—scarce.

"Don't get too cute."

"Seriously, how did God come to the decision that after making humans, He would expose us to this?"

"Finally, a reasonable question. God didn't make this place for humans. He made this place for our lord and his angels. They were thrown out of heaven. Well, where to throw them? I guess He couldn't throw them out of heaven unless there was somewhere other than heaven.

"Now, we know Satan tried to overtake heaven, so we can assume God probably wasn't thinking of the Bahamas when He was creating hell. Well, since it was to be a place for God's enemies to go, it probably lacked excellent status. Now God has banished all of his enemies to this place of horror; it is important that it be a place of extreme horror, to keep other angels from ever considering rebellion.

"God created Adam. He so loved Adam that He didn't want him to be alone. So

God created Eve, to be a mate for Adam. It is important to know that God loved Adam so much that He decided to give him a gift, which man has never understood. You see, If God would have made Adam with no free will, then Adam would have been the same as an elaborate toy. He would have done everything he was programmed to do and turned off every night and turned back on in the morning and said whatever God programmed him to say. God said, 'I will give this man the gift of free will. The gift to choose. This will be a gift I will never take back. He will always have the freedom of choice. I will instruct him and he will choose to obey Me or suffer the consequences.' What God did was not just create something that could move, walk, and talk, but He created something that was actually an independent, free-thinking mortal, capable of making his own decisions.

"God, in His wisdom, looked at the prospect of man and said, 'For Me to give man this freedom, I must surrender my control over him.' God then concluded for one to truly own something, you first must let it go. If it comes back to you, it is yours. If it doesn't, it is not. God knew Satan would tempt man, but God loved His creation enough that He was willing to part with the ones who wouldn't come back for the joy of the ones who would praise Him and bring Him honor and glory. So God made man and then surrendered him to the world.

"Not long after man was on the earth, Satan tempted Eve, and through the woman was able to lure the man into sin. God, in His morning of man's failure, was asked by Satan if the ones who rebelled against God, as Satan did, would be condemned to the same place. As Satan knew, God being perfect, He couldn't let one group of rebels go free while the others suffered. So God said all of the rebels will be cast down into Hell.

"I'm sure you heard that when Eve was approached by Satan, he was in the form of a snake. This was just one of many forms he could take. Satan was lord of the earth. He was the high ruler. When Moses tried to take the people out of Egypt, he ran into a lot of problems. Had God not accompanied him, he would have died. As a manner of fact, Satan could do miracles on the earth just like God. When Moses threw down his staff and it turned into a serpent, the Pharaoh had his magicians throw down their staffs, and they became serpents as well. When Moses turned the water into blood, so did the Pharaoh's magicians. Satan commanded great power. We could enslave people on the earth by physical means. We could appear before them through manifestations and control them. Then a terrible thing happened.

"There was an announcement. We were ready. King Herod blew it. All he had to do was kill one baby. One little baby boy. We knew in advance what town He would be born in. We knew the approximate date. Somehow the baby Jesus was born and grew up to fulfill all the prophecies made about him. Satan had forty days to try and defeat Him. It didn't happen. The Dark Angels had no idea what the death of Jesus meant. It has been rumored that Satan himself didn't know what the ramifications of Jesus' blood meant."

"What did it mean?"

"When Jesus died, He didn't go to heaven. He didn't lie there in the tomb. He descended to—you guessed it—'Hell.' Well, needless to say Satan wasn't real happy. To hear them tell it, Satan wasn't prepared at all. Just like that, Jesus came through the front door. All these little Christians keep talking about Jesus, the Lamb of God. Well, let me tell you something. What came through that chasm wasn't a lamb. If you think CHIRZPA was loud, guess again. The ones who were here say there was an explosion. There stood Jesus with a white robe on that was so bright no one could look on Him. There were four Beings with him. They all had six wings with eyes on the wings. They had these tremendous bodies and one had the head of a man, one had the head of a lion, one had the head of a ox, and one had the head of an eagle. Nothing in all of hell could come near them. They say one stroke of their mighty wings would blow out hell's fires. Then Jesus took over. That's right—how many of those Christians would croak if they knew Jesus actually ran hell for three days? During those three days, the one who is supposed to be the 'lamb' broke all of our earthly power implements. We had nothing left. He literally broke the chains of hell. The very implements we used to inflict people."

"What do you mean, He broke the chains of hell?"

"What I'm saying is, after Jesus and His bodyguards created mayhem for three days, He left and ascended to the earth. From there he ascended up to heaven. What he managed to do for us is render us powerless against the people of the earth. We once could manifest ourselves in different ways and control people. He took all our great toys away. Now all we can do is make suggestions to them through the orb."

"What about witches and demons? We still have those things available, don't we?"

"Sorry—all those things are currently not at our disposal. There are still witches and we have demons, but not with the power they had before Jesus came. As we approach the end of times, we will regain these implements. We will have our full power again."

"Well, then what are all these people talking about when they say they know somebody who can cast out demons? And everybody knows there are still witches around. I saw a special on them once."

"Oh, boy, you saw a special. Well, Pervert, when Jesus left hell, he broke the power Satan had on the earth. I hate to tell you this, but there ain't no Santa Claus. Demons or witches don't have the power they once had on the earth. You can be possessed by evil. You can have a very weak character and let yourself go into areas of evil. But facts are facts. Jesus came through here and broke the chains of sin. Before, we had you. We had real power. Now all a person has to do is acknowledge God and His Son Jesus. What everybody down here didn't understand is the power of the blood of Jesus. When they spilled Jesus' blood it was, for lack of a better definition, magical. His blood covered every sin with one exception—not believing that God exists. So the way it works is to activate the blood of Jesus, or as we would say it down here, to have power over the principalities of evil, to be forgiven of the sin committed. Can the magical potion accomplish all? The calling up of the all-powerful formula? This is the blood of Jesus. All those Christians have to do is ask for forgiveness in the name of Jesus, and their sin is washed clean.

"What a drag! We can't whip up a demon. We can't fly in a witch. We can't even put a curse on them. You see, Jesus broke all our power when he died."

"You told me there are more people going to hell now than any other time. So what good did Jesus dying on the cross do? What good is His blood if idiots like me never figure it out?" I am stunned.

"Well, Pervert, it goes something like this. God surrendered His control over man, giving them the ultimate power to choose. So as only the wisdom of God could figure out, the only way for man to come back to God is through surrender. God surrendered control of man to man. In order for man to come back to God, man has to surrender to God. The only way man can surrender to God is, without seeing, hearing, or touching God, man has to believe in Him. Not only in Him, but in His Son Jesus."

"What does that have to do with surrender?" I ask.

"You can't accept God and His Son Jesus without surrender. You have to surrender your own self as God did. He gave up His control. He never asked you to do anything He didn't do. He will be your God, if you will surrender to Him. You have to be willing to put Him first. That means you can no longer be self-serving. So in order to do that, you must surrender all the basic desires of your heart. God first, others second. To receive Jesus as your Lord, you have to die."

"What?"

"That's right, you have to let your old self die. You must give up your old life of putting yourself first. You might say, 'How could Jesus ask me to give up my life for Him?' Well, He gave up His life for you. So He, just as God, didn't ask you to do anything He hasn't already done for you. When He died on the cross, it was for you, idiot. So now no demons can keep you from a relationship with God. Jesus' promise to you was, if you want a personal relationship with God, you've got it. All you have to do is start listening to God, read the Bible, and start talking to Him, through prayer. The secret to prayer, what non-Christians don't know, is so simple, Pervert. All you have to do is at the end of your prayer to God, just say 'In Jesus' name' and because of His blood, you have a direct line to God. What a country! Imagine, though you started out with a perfectly clean soul, you managed to screw it up. Even so, if you would have been just half as smart as a fool, you would have realized that Jesus paid the price so you could be forgiven. Even you, Pervert, could have been forgiven, and stand in front of the Almighty clean, white as snow, washed by the blood of Jesus. But not you, rebel. It was those bad choices," he titters.

"What good would having a direct line to God have done me? I turned my back on God, and as you said earlier, God turned His back on me," I mutter.

"Oh, that's sad, Pervert. 'I turned my back on God, and He turned his back on me.' That's why you are such a loser. You never looked for answers. You always looked for excuses. The truth is all you had to do was to accept Jesus as your Lord and Savior and ask God to forgive you. At that very moment, you would have been white as snow."

"How would I have known? Would I have felt different? Would a bright light appear in front of me? Would a voice speak to me from the ceiling? 'Your ticket has been punched and your fare paid.'"

"Cute. There's not doubt you are in the right place."

"Well? How would I have known I was forgiven?" I protest.

"For the first time I understand. The way God evaluates potential candidates for heaven is with a single measure.

"Speak plainly, Eluder. What does that mean?"

"The measure of a soul is faith. Like you said, how would you know God forgave you? Well, the only way you would know is through your faith in His word."

"What kinda junk…."

"Shut up, Pervert. This is pure genius. God, once again, with all His wisdom pulled the wool over the eyes of even the brightest minds. He created a measure to get into heaven. Then He just moved back and let it happen." He howls. "How magnificent!"

"What are you raving about, Eluder?"

"The only way you can know, as you so elegantly pointed out, that God has forgiven you is by faith. What does that mean? It means, Pervert, that you must read God's word and then not only read it, but also believe it. You see, to have faith in something, you have to believe in it. Right?"

"Right."

"There it is. The Catch-22! You had never read God's word, nor had you listened to someone tell you about it. So for you to accept the fact that you were forgiven was impossible. You are where you are supposed to be. Jesus' blood did you no good. Because even if you would have been desperate enough to call out to God and ask Him to forgive you of all your sins, even if you somehow had known that you had to ask it in Jesus' name, it still would have done you no good. Why? Because you didn't know the Lord is your God, and, therefore, you wouldn't have any faith that it would happen.

"You see, you have to know something about something before you believe in it. Even the shoes you wore. You bought certain types of shoes because you knew they would fit. You had faith in them because of your previous experience with that brand. You knew the brand name, and you felt comfortable buying that brand. You had faith. But if someone came to you and offered to take those shoes and give you a pair with a brand you had never heard of, you would have said?"

"No way!"

"Exactly, you would have said 'no way', just as you would have said in your heart if someone would have said, 'You have been forgiven of all your sins'. Man! What revelation! God calls the Christians His children. Get it? They're like family. They are His children because they know Him. If a father calls his child, the child comes running. Why? Because the child knows the father. The child trusts the father. The child has faith in the father. How many times have you seen a child jump from a safe place into possible harm, at the beckoning of his father? Why? The child has complete faith in the father.

"The pain of it all, Pervert, is only a child of the heavenly Father knows the Father well enough to trust Him just on His word. So when a Christian reads the Father's word, it assures the child of forgiveness. Then the child accepts the Father's word on faith, therefore, believing it to be so. Something you could not do."

"I never had a chance."

"God created a measure that eliminates all the multitudes that put themselves first. The agony is, we did it to ourselves. What's that old saying—'Give them enough rope and they'll hang themselves'. Think about it, Pervert. The rules are in play. The choices are yours. There are no excuses. You either are a child of the living God or you are not. There is no middle ground. The ingenuous, yet brilliance of it all."

"So you're saying this master plan means there are no excuses?"

"Right."

"So God's immaculate plan is you and your family had access to the truth. God was there for my family and me. Jesus' blood was spilt for my family and me. The forgiveness was there for us as well. All we had to do was accept it. By not accepting it, we rejected it. Therefore, we got what we deserved."

"Right."

"This stinks!"

"Right."

"Why have you told me all of this? What good does it do me? Do I have a chance to escape this horrible place? Will I get another chance'?"

"Sorry. No more chances. All of your chances were in life. The same as all the rest of us."

"Then why have you tormented me with these facts? What possible good are they?"

"I'm not sure. I thought when you came to me something was wrong. I wasn't sure what it was. I'm still not 100 percent sure. I have known someone was watching us, recording what we say.

"Who? I don't see anybody."

"Until recently I thought it was AVTOTAR, the one who listens. I saw AVTOTAR pass across the way by the center line of the orbs, so now I know it is not he who is listening."

"Well, then, who is it?"

"I don't know. All I know is there is an observer present. Why they are interested in someone as pitiful as you, I don't know. Who knows? Maybe your story will be heard after all. I don't know if it will be played here or up there, but something or someone is listening and recording everything you do."

"What do you mean, me?"

"This entity was not here before you came, and it will leave when you leave."

"How do you know that?"

"I just know."

"That's weird. Maybe they are monitoring us to make sure we are not plotting against them."

"Give it a rest, Pervert. They don't care what you are plotting. If you don't do the job, you get an invitation from guess who. He puts the ol' talons in you and down you go."

"Then what can it be?"

"Maybe it's from Idiots R Us, and it's here for a pickup."

"Okay. I get it. Who is next on the Aethyr list?" I ask.

"ZIP, Aethyr for those who are not."

"Great, I thought you were going to say 'as in code'. Get it? Zip code?"

"ZIP is your kind of Aethyr. He is there to reinforce the feelings of those who are downtrodden. Those who have never been given a chance. Those just like you, loser. The ones with the excuses."

"Give me an example of someone other than me."

"ZIP, during a special hearing, told of how many minorities he is able to comfort. One of the prime reasons for not performing up to one's capabilities. Diversion. You know, 'I could have, if it weren't for the color of my skin.' 'I never had a chance because we were poor.' 'My dad was an alcoholic.' 'My mother was a slut.' 'My older brother got everything.' 'My mother loved her more than me.' ZIP calls it, 'the name it and claim it league'. All you have to do is pick your excuse. My mother didn't'....My father didn't....or any other thing you want. The secret is never look at someone like Helen Keller. It rea1ly screws up your defense. We like entitlement. ZIP said the last thing we want are people feeling with God's help they can make it. We prefer them to constantly search for some complaint. You see, if we can keep them focused on what somebody should be doing for them, then they won't be looking for ways to do it for themselves."

"Well, from what I've seen, we don't have anything to worry about."

"That was true ten years ago. There is a movement among the black leaders in the United States. Unlike the past voice that was calling for more government aid, the new black leaders are calling for the men in their communities to stand up and be accountable, to get off government programs and go to work. To start becoming responsible parents. To pay child support, if they have a child outside their home. To raise their children with moral values. This is creating quite a ruckus around here. They are starting to have role models like Colin Powell, Reverend Myles Monroe, and Reggie Jackson. Black men who have made it on their own. Men who fear God. Men who don't cower to political correctness.

"This is such an issue that ZIP has joined forces with another Aethyr to try and combat this new dilemma. POP, Aethyr of division, has united with ZIP. Never before have they joined forces. To divide is to conquer. We are starting to hear black men and Hispanic men say they are American first, black or Hispanic next. This is a terrible thing. We have been making great progress from the sixties until recently. Something is changing. We are not sure what is causing this change. We know we have to do something to stop this unification. Some of our best progress has been accomplished with the black leaders. In the past they have kept division in the country by continually whining about the black man's plight. ZIP and POP are launching a massive campaign to get the old black leaders back in the public eye. These new leaders and their responsibility song and dance are killing us."

"Hey, we are safe. The black man isn't going to float his own boat. He will be crying about the injustices done to him and his ancestry for many more years," I offer.

The Eluder snarls. "Don't count on it. If that were true, ZIP and POP wouldn't be launching the campaign I just mentioned. It's a little scary. The United States has this freedom of religion act that just kicks our butt. They are the true strongholds of the religious community. We have been able to erode it for the last seventy-five years, but we are seeing a comeback in the younger generation. They are finding God and dropping the racial hatred. We have the TV media helping us in every way. They are using profanity on the air. We have the daytime entertainment where they bring in the lowest class people they can find to do the most absurd things they can think of. I mean, we have the networks in our pocket. The movie industry is actually more concerned about garbage than the TV networks. But still, more and more people are finding God, and we need to find a new divider.

"Well, ZIP has his hands full with all the little whiners out there saying, 'My mommy made me eat wheat bread, and now I'm allergic to anything with wheat. My daddy yelled at me when I was ten and traumatized me. Now I can't function because I'm so confused about my relationship with my father'."

Laughingly, I add, "Hey, I know people like that."

"Yeah, everybody wants an excuse for being a jerk. It's a greater thing the mothers and fathers do for their children allowing themselves to be the sole reason for why their children aren't happy. Whatever the children do, they should never look in the mirror. They might see the real problem. 'Oh, no! That's why I'm not happy! It's that jerk in the mirror'!" He cackles.

"So are there any other Aethyrs?"

"ZAX. Aethyr of the one with a great name. ZAX is continually reminding the nobles of their duty to the family. The family can and, in most cases, does become greater than any other entity. This is important. If people of great wealth and power are not distracted by internal problems, they can do much good. So ZAX must apply the family pressure. It makes some go off the deep end. This is important because it keeps the others distracted. They are busy trying to save the family name, which they value so highly. Remember, Pervert, divide and conquer. So ZAX will tell the one who broke under pressure that the family name is more important to the others than he or she is. Beautiful, huh? Also, there is the one to whom the family name has brought attention. This person is encouraged to embrace their name as a lover would their partner. Then, at the first sign of exposing the family name as something other than what it has always appeared, this person becomes enraged as though you had yanked the covers off them while with their lover. Then there is the duty-bound person, the one who feels the moral obligation to maintain the family, to keep his chin up, no manner what ship enters the harbor. This person can be removed from God simply by forcing him to choose between righteousness and family. Works every time."

"Well, I'll have to admit I don't relate to that one. I don't think anyone who is in charge will assign me to a great name."

"You're quite right."

"So, who else is left?" I ask.

"ICH, Aethyr of tension. If you can't take the heat, get out of the kitchen. Well, it sounds good, but it's not that simple. All these people are running around on planet earth. Let's see, there are those who have jobs they don't like. There are those who have spouses they don't love, and in lots of cases, don't like. There are those who have family they don't like, those who have friends they don't like, those that have cars they don't like, those who have homes they don't…."

"Yeah, yeah, I got it. There is a lot of stuff one is around that one might not like."

"ICH is there to promote the irritation that occurs when you don't like it. Now, what comes into play is, how long does one let ICH play his music? Do they immediately turn him off, using self-control and rebuking him, or do they listen to him and say to themselves, 'Yeah, yeah. Why me? Why does this happen to me?' Then ICH usually goes for the shoulders and neck. His favorite places. Inflict that pain, baby. Sock it to 'em. In many cases ICH can keep enough tension on them so they have to eliminate whatever it is they feel is causing it."

"Hold on. Hold on," I question. "To eliminate what is causing the tension is a good thing, isn't it? I mean, what better thing could a person do? I heard the shrinks talking about stress relieving all the time. They were always telling the people to locate the area of the stress and then see if it were possible to eliminate it. Right?"

"Right, wonder boy. That's what they said. By the way, you did believe what the good doctors told you, didn't you?"

"Of course. Wasn't I supposed to?"

"In keeping with your philosophy, I think it paramount you believe the psychologist. Since psychology isn't an exact science, Pervert, what do you think that means?"

"They haven't figured everything out yet?"

"Well…that's right, Einstein. So if they haven't, as you say, figured everything out yet, then why would you accept what they say as fact?"

"Because they knew a lot more than I did?"

"A lot more about what?"

"A lot more about the human mind."

"Did they know a lot more about your 'mind' than you did?"

"Is that a trick question?"

"Who would know more about what your thoughts are than you?"

"Well, they ask you leading questions…you know?"

"Questions leading you where?"

"Questions leading you to answers."

"Who has the answers?"

"Hey. I see where this is going."

"Good. A psychologist is like masseuse. They are okay if you have the money. If not, you can accomplish the same thing with a little thought or a little exercise.

"Man, you're a hard dude."

"Your creator made you with all the answers inside, not outside. If someone has the money, and they want to indulge themselves, that's great. Go for it. But to go to a psychologist as though you were going to a physician is in contrast with what the word of God says. First you would need to find out if the psychologist is a Christian. If he is a Christian, then there is a chance he/she can help you. If he claims to be a Christian, then he has probably read God's word. If not, he is of no use to you. God's word is truth. You can shake it, bake it or stir it all around, but His word keeps coming out on top.

"This is one of the great campaigns ICH has going at the present. We have all these PhDs in psychology telling people they are right to feel the way they feel. They get paid big bucks to agree with the wealthy. Isn't that wonderful? This means the chances of these people finding God are almost impossible. We have these idiots sitting in these chairs saying things like, 'Tell me more,' and 'How does that make you feel?' ' Maybe you were abused as a child and didn't know it.' 'If it doesn't feel good, then don't do it.' Boy! I love this stuff."

"People don't pay someone for that kind of garbage. They pay them to help them work out their problems so they can relieve the tension in their lives."

"Have you ever gone to a psychologist?"

"No."

"If they don't know the truth, how can they guide you to it? Are you saying they just say soothing things to make someone feel better for the moment?"

"I don't know. Let me ask you a question. How could someone spend the time required to get a degree — I mean a PhD in something, and not be able to help or guide someone without those credentials to a level of peace?"

The Eluder snickers. "Do you think because someone has a degree from a college they know the truth? Who do you think are teaching these courses? These new ideas are things man has thought up, things they have pondered and come to a conclusion, that if it sounds good to their ears and to their colleagues, then it's probable. That is all it has to be, 'probable,' when you are talking about something that is not an exact science. Then some professor will publish it and there you go. Isn't that great? To hell with the truth. What a country! They have the word of God available (the Bible) to them, by definition, the 'Truth,' and yet they are listening to men who ponder and conclude. 'Hey, baby, we are on a roll!'

"Can't you see? JCH stated that if people with great tension are led by people without the answers, then the tension gets greater and greater. They start to drown. They go to the shrinks more often trying to get help. What a master plan! They keep going back to the very people who are adding to the confusion, thereby contributing to the tension."

"You mean all psychologists are frauds?"

"Of course not. There are Christian counselors. There are also psychologists who were good students. They really want to help, but they don't know God. These are our best people. They serve us well. You can't beat that sincerity," the Eluder titters, "someone who is really trying to get to the truth. The problem is, they may not know it when they hear it. They try so hard. They stay late at the office. They go back through all the information they have, all the case studies. Who could ever accuse them of deception? No, these are our best soldiers. Tension is very important. If we allow these people to relieve the tension, there would be a great danger. Tension is distracting. End of story. Keep someone distracted, and you keep him from personal growth, self-help, which eventually could possibly lead to helping others."

"Now, that makes sense. Keep them thinking about themselves, then while drowning they can't help someone else," I offer.

"Hey, kid. You might make it yet."

"Give me another one.

"LOE, the first Aethyr of glory. LOE is connected at the hip with all things of glory. LOE said when glory comes to a person, only those grounded in God can handle it. You need only look at the movie stars and some highly successful people.

The best part of glory is it just doesn't get the immediate recipient but also most of the people close to them. The gift that just keeps on giving." He mocks, "You would think that someone who has achieved great fame and fortune would be living a great life, experiencing all the wonderful things money can buy. With this new ID, one would think they would be associating with the best of the best. But the truth screams out in Proverbs 27:19: *A mirror reflects a man's face, but what he* is *really like is shown by the kind of friends he chooses.*"

"Yeah, that makes sense. Everybody wants to be around people they can relate to."

"You've got it. When you're on top of the world, you're not looking for God. So this group doesn't require much attention."

"To hell with the glorious people. What else do you have in your bag?"

'ZIM is Aethyr of application."

"The Aethyr of application? Application?"

"Hold on, Pervert. You were doing so well. What do you feel was your best talent? Deep down inside, if things had gone just the right way, what was your number one talent?"

"That's tough. I guess it could have been public speaking. I mean, I always had a gift when it came to making a point."

"And what did you do with it?"

"What do you mean?"

"If that was a talent God gave you, then what did you do with it?"

"I never felt the confidence to try and apply myself"

"In retrospect, is there regret?"

"Yes. Loads of it."

"Then you can thank ZIM. The magic word is 'apply'. You said you didn't apply yourself. Well, guess who encouraged you to procrastinate? And here's ZIM." He giggles.

"You mean he was that little voice in my head saying, 'Why would they want you?'"

"Well, well, you identified him. Good for you. Now can you see how important he is? Yes. His encouragement to procrastinate keeps people from ever attaining their potential, leaving them with disappointment and sadness. And don't forget hopelessness, a real key in demoralizing someone." He cackles again.

"I don't find that funny, Eluder!"

"Oh, gee, does everything have to be about you, Pervert?"

"If I had only known, I could have done something with my life."

"While you were on earth you had choices, Pervert. Now you have two. You do what is expected of you to the degree of excellence, or you go to the place of desolation, where there are no more choices. The beauty of this place is, Pervert, nobody cares what you choose. Nobody cares where you go. You turned your back on the only one who cared. So get over it."

"You're right as always. Tell me, what other groups does ZIM concentrate on?"

"Hey, Daddy wants you to go to college and make something of yourself. Of course Mommy and Daddy never spent much time helping you to find your niche in life. They never insisted you get summer jobs or work part-time to find out what it's like in the real world. They just want you to get a college degree. Then they can feel all warm and snuggly about how they gave you all the help you needed to be a success. So what does the mighty ZIM do? He does the same thing he did to you. He tells them not to go for the thing way down their heart. He creates a lot of confusion. Then these people go off to college, and not having a clue what they want to do, they either fail miserably or come home with a degree that doesn't mean jack squat.

"The beauty of this is, in most cases, it creates a rift between the parents and the child. The parents feel cheated because their child didn't do well in the workplace. The child feels the disappointment and withdraws. Is this great, or what? We actually use the parents love and desire to help their children and the children's desire to please the parents and turn it into disillusionment. Look at how brilliant our plans are! These people with good intentions going about their business every day without any idea that we are working, preparing, and devising all these masterful ways to keep them from their eternal reward. That's right, boys and girls, they'll be spending that vacation at the beautiful and 'always warm' beaches of Hades coming to you real soon." He laughs. "Don't you just love it? These people are tucked away in their cozy homes saying things like, 'How fortunate we are to live in a country like this.' 'To have a home like this and live in the land of opportunity'. Little do they know. If they could only visit us, my boy, they would live in a third world country in a cardboard box if it meant they would find the Lord and wouldn't have to come here. Let them have their illusions of grandeur. It won't be long and they too will receive their invitation from Beelzebub. 'Greetings. You have been pre-accepted to the Order of the Abyss, located at the bottomless pit. Lucifer and his staff welcome you'." He snickers.

"Hey, what's up? They look like they're coming our way."

"Don't speak again, Pervert. The one on the right is AVTOTAR, he who listens. He may have been what I felt earlier. The one on the left is ADVOPT, she who silently watches. The one in the middle is PABNIXP, the one who governs.

PABNIXP speaks. 'Eluder, you have been accused of disobedient behavior. How do you plead?"

"Honorable PABNIXP, I know not of what you speak," the Eluder quietly says.

"It has been brought to our attention by AVTOTAR and ADVOPT that you have told the Pervert of Jesus' reign in hell, that you spoke of how Jesus overcame our forces of darkness, that He broke the chains of hell that were binding to the citizens of earth, that we no longer possess the power to reign over the earth as we once did. Is this true?"

"Honorable PABNIXP, as you know, AVTOTAR and ADVOPT would never distort the truth. Therefore I am defenseless."

'LAPARIN, protector of men, what are you doing here'?" asks PABNIXP.

"I am here on behalf of Pervert, who has not completed the transformation to Eluder. Therefore, he stands innocent."

PABNIXP agrees.

"Eluder, you are in violation of our secret trust."

Just then that same evil being that was taking the man screaming down to the......

The Eluder cries out, “Ohhhh! Wait!”

VSNARDA is grasping him with his hand. His talons are piercing the Eluder’s side. I see the pain in his face and the fear in his eyes.

“PABNIXP, you are of the Aethyr BAG, Aethyr of doubt! He knows my work. I beg you to ask him for my stay,” cries the Eluder.

“Hold it, VSNARDA! You mean BAG will know you, Eluder?”

“Just remind him of the great sitting on skepticism. The Eluder who gave the examples that pleased him.”

PABNIXP announces, ‘No one is to move.”

Now he is gone. Just gone! There is a weird-looking mass where he was. It looks like an energy field. My Lord, he is back, just that fast.

PABNIXP commands, “Release the Eluder.”

VSNARDA squeezes the Eluder and you can hear a pop, and his eyes roll back in his head.

PABNIXP charges, “Release the Eluder now!”

As VSNARDA pulls his talons from the Eluder’s chest and stomach, he falls. As he lies here, a darkness falls over the area. It is a Dark Angel!

The Dark Angel probes, “Who has injured the Eluder?”

PABNIXP utters, “VSNARDA was told to release him.”

“And....”

PABNIXP responds, “Well, as you can see, he decided to give him a squeeze before obeying.”

The Dark Angel sneers, “PABNIXP, VSNARDA, come with me!”

The Dark Angel is holding out his hand and the Eluder’s body starts to move, like the molecules in his body are being rearranged. Now the Eluder stands up. The others exit the area. The area we are in is like a cave with a great opening. At the opening we can see the endless number of orbs. The beings who are coming and going are not walking but just gliding through the air.

The Eluder says, “Well, that was close. Good thing I did so well in the session BAG gave or it would be a hot time tonight.”

“Man, that VSNARDA is one bad being!”

“Nothing personal,” remarks the Eluder. “He performs a service. However, he will get to feel some pain on this day.”

‘How is that possible?”

“When a Dark Angel tells you to come go with him, it’s not because he wants to socialize with you.”

“I guess VSNARDA was planning on taking you to....”

“The place of Desolation. It’s not his fault. By definition, VSNARDA is he who casts down, into the depths. That’s what he does.”

“You said he?”

“Best guess.”

“Tell me more about the place of desolation.”

“Well, you are given the opportunity to see the area as often as you like. Our lord feels it helps keep you focused. So one of the things you might find interesting is the thing that was the major contributor to bringing you here is what determines your location and circumstances there."

"What does that mean?"

"For example, you have a big mouth. This is what they told you when you came in, correct?"

"Correct."

'Then here is where you will be placed."

Suddenly there is a hologram-type image in front of us, once again showing the place of desolation.

"See the people to the right of center?"

'Yes. The ones who seem in great pain and appear to be screaming, but nothing is coming out of their mouths?" I offer.

"This is because as VSNARDA drops them off; they are greeted by NABAOMI, he who knows pain. NABAOMI then rips their tongues out of their mouth. So the thing that kept them out of heaven is no longer a problem. On earth there was still hope for them. Until they moved into eternity, there was always hope, the hope they would find God and change their lives. But once they arrive here, there is no more hope. So our lord rectifies the problem. In this case a person with a big mouth, someone who is continually wagging his tongue, has it removed. Now they aren't a diversion. On earth people like you were considered a distraction. You didn't do anything great, nor did you do anything inauspicious. You just continually brought attention to yourself. On earth you were tolerable because of the hope factor. However, here that factor no longer applies."

"So Satan rips their tongues out?"

"Yes, that's why they look as though they are in pain, because they are in pain. And the reason they appear to be screaming is because they are screaming. You can't hear them because they don't have a tongue. But if you listen closely, you can hear a gurgle," he laughs angrily.

"Why? Why is it this way?"

"Well, it really makes sense if you think about it. To get to heaven, you must be humble. So what kept you from being humble? Pride. That's right, pride. So what was it that distracted you from achieving the goal you wished you had achieved? Your pride in what? Whatever the answer is, that's what our lord is going to remove.

"When you were on earth you had hope. That meant you could change. You could submit to God and He would be your God and Jesus would be your Lord. So you would have given up your old ways. You would have stopped running your mouth. You would have put God before yourself. Ah, that means you would have submitted to God's will rather than your own. So instead of drawing attention to yourself, you would yield yourself to God's word, the Bible, and avoid doing things that bring attention to yourself. Instead you would have given God and Jesus the glory. This would have meant you chose to use your gift, as a gift from God, for God. But in your case, as those poor souls down there, the choice was made to use the gift to bring honor to you. This is not acceptable to God, nor is it acceptable to Satan. God allows you the opportunity to use your gift to honor Him. Satan removes the gift because a gift brings joy, and those who are cast down are not allowed joy."

"Give me another example."

"Okay, those who are proud of their intellectual prowess, the people who didn't accept God because they were too smart to fall for a book that was authored by humans. They were always coming up with questions they thought were brilliant. Questions like, 'If there is a God, then how could He let a baby die?' 'How could He let so many bad things happen?' Some of them even go so far as to reinvent God."

"What do you mean 'reinvent God'?"

"These people are a direct controversy. They say they don't believe in God. They say they don't believe the Bible is the word of God. But these poor confused people—excuse me, these brilliant people—say things like, 'I believe some of the Bible.' 'I believe there is a God, but I don't think He is as the Bible and all the prophets say He is.' 'My God is a forgiving God and would never punish anyone.'

"How about that, sports fans! A genius. That's right. Step right up to the podium. genius. You just invented a god. Why, you are so smart, all you have to do is just say something, and it becomes true. You say the Bible isn't God's word and so be it. You say God wouldn't punish someone for turning his or her back on Him, and suddenly a new god comes floating down from heaven. You say you believe in this wonderful God, but you don't believe in hell. Boy, are they in for a shock!"

'Well, if Satan is going to rip my tongue out, what is he going to do to these people?"

"You want to see?"

The area opens up again. This hologram, for lack of a better definition, is at the entrance to the area. We are in an area much like a cave with a large opening about twenty feet high and about forty feet wide. When he says, "Let's look," the entire mouth of the cave is filled with the hologram.

"Do you see the labyrinth?"

"Do you mean that maze?" I ask.

"Yes. What do you see?"

"I see people wandering around, going in and out of areas. It looks as though every time they choose a door, it's the wrong one. They seem to be confused and bewildered. They seem to be making all bad decisions. They look completely unraveled. They all look so miserable."

"Well, those are the people who considered themselves intellects. They are doomed to the labyrinth. They find that their intelligence fails them. They are made aware of how puny and ignorant they really are. The universe is so far beyond their comprehension that they are utterly rendered insignificant. However, this is not a lesson for the day, nor is it a crash course. This is an exercise for all eternity."

"Do you mean these people will wander around this maze, going in and out of doors where they get struck down, humiliated, and ridiculed forever'?"

"Yes. Remember that on earth this was their gift. They could have used it to explain God's word. Instead they chose to dispute God's word. So Satan has rendered them harmless. They will never get out of the labyrinth. They will spend eternity trying to find a way out. Each time they use their intelligence to choose a path, they are thwarted. Now the very thing that gave them an exaggerated confidence has become their nemesis."

"So you are saying if they had used their intelligence to promote God, they wouldn't be here?"

"Right. If they had served God, giving others comfort in their wisdom and knowledge by explaining portions of the Bible to those who had difficulty in understanding, then they would have been acquitted."

"Maybe they needed someone to explain it to them."

"You are either a part of the problem or a part of the solution, either for or against. The people in the labyrinth are there because they were against God. There are always choices. These people made their own choices. They chose to deny God. They turned their back on Jesus and God. They are in their just place."

"How could anybody, once given a choice, choose this place over heaven? No one would do that. I still say this isn't right."

"The people who burned to death in that old apartment building down the street from you weren't responsible for the fire, but they burned to death just the same."

"What does that mean?"

"It means they knew the building was old, but the rent was cheap. They knew the old man who lived downstairs smoked and drank too much. But the price was right, and it would be a pain to move. Well, you could say they weren't responsible for their death. Some might say they could have prevented their death by moving, calling attention to the problem on the first floor by planning an escape route in case of a fire. The young couple on the third floor with the two small children moved out because of the drunk who smoked. Was it fate that determined who lived and who died?"

"Why is it some people make good decisions and others don't?"

"That's a complicated question. It requires a multifarious answer. You see, when the Bible refers to the sins of the father, and his sins being a curse for three generations, well, most people don't get it. When the head of the house sins, it affects everyone in the house."

"How do you mean it affects everyone?"

"Well, look at the first earthly father, Adam. He sinned. His son Cain killed his other son Abel. This was caused from the curse on Adam, but the curse went beyond Adam to the family."

"So the reason some people have it bad is because of their father?"

"Or their grandfather."

"I need an example, Eluder. I don't know if I can buy this one."

"One, the father isn't a Christian. He doesn't go by Christian teachings that say, for example, one must refrain from going in debt. So he is constantly in over his head. He buys things he can't afford. He has to let things go back because he can't make the payments. What do you think the son will do in his household when he is in charge? Two, the father drinks in excess. Therefore he never attends any functions because he is drunk. The few he does attend his children wish had never happened. He embarrasses them to tears. Do you think his children are going to be well-adjusted, socially active adults? Three, the father is dishonest. He will say whatever he feels necessary to get what he wants. What do you think his children will do? Four, the father beats the mother. The children run and hide, but they see. What to you think his children will do when they are grown? Five, the father cheats on the mother. The children are ridiculed at school. Their friends hear how their father behaves. Do you think that will affect the children? Six, the father is like you. All he wants is to get lucky. He doesn't want to be a father. He just wants to sleep with that cute little thing who works in accounting. So he finally convinces her that his intentions are honorable and eventually after many dates and events, she gives in and sleeps with him. About a month later she tells the man who told her all the things she wanted to hear that she is pregnant. Bear with me. I know you aren't going to believe this, but that guy who told her how much he loved children, how he wanted to settle down one day, well, that guy won't even speak to her now. She has a choice. Get an abortion or be a single parent. What do you think the child will grow up to be?

"The sins of a father are far greater that most imagine. Most men today think it's the women's responsibility. They say to themselves in the corner in the dark, like the rats they really are, 'If she wouldn't have pulled her pants down, she wouldn't have had the problem.' 'All I was doing was following my natural urges.' What the hell kind of answer is that? The men of this time are coming to us at a rate faster than a speeding bullet. Can you imagine? Fathering a child and never accepting the responsibility of caring for it? Never allowing the child the right to be able to say, 'This is my dad'? Never giving the child the security of knowing Daddy is in the next room? I know we are protected. No, the children in the US are saying. 'My mother is a loose woman and my dad was a one-night stand'. This child can't say, 'Here's my dad,' but can only hear the negative things the mother has to say about the no-good bum.' And yet this worthless piece of dung is walking around somewhere with his head held high, full of false pride. Instead of his face in his hands, weeping over some little child out there fatherless, he's looking for action."

"Guys don't think like that."

'What are you saying? God told you that you could only have one organ so you didn't get a brain?"

"No, I'm saying, men just don't think about those kind of things."

"Men who had solid fathers who were Christian men and taught their children right from wrong and to think about those things. So this brings us back to the problem of sin. How does sin affect generations? Well, just as soon as a young man becomes a rebel, he breaks away from his parents. This is the beginning of the separation from God. Then come his descendants. How were they raised? Did the rebel mature fast enough to get back in the church before his children were born? If not, then what curses did he pass to his children? The one curse that is synonymous with rebellion is pride. They are inseparable. Where you find one, you will always find the other. In Proverbs 8:13 is this message: *If anyone respects and fears God, he will hate evil. For wisdom hates pride, arrogance, corruption and deceit of every kind.*

"Notice what was number one on the hit list, pride. Arrogance runs a close second. We know to get to heaven one must be humble. Well, you can't have it both ways. You are humble or you are proud."

"Yeah, but do you have the choice as to which you are going to be? I mean, you are made one way or the other! Right?"

"Wrong. You are exactly who you want to be."

"Bull—nobody is who they want to be."

"I am referring to character."

"That's not right. We all aspire to be more than we are. Yet circumstances cause us to make concessions."

"That is a twenty-first century American copout."

"Where do you get that's a copout?"

"Listen, you little frail and fragile thing. Life is made up of choices. Do you think the guy who is a priest is someone who has never been tempted? Do you think the guy who plays professional sports is someone with a gift, who loves to work out, and is lucky?"

"I understand that a priest is tempted and the athlete has to work hard."

"It all starts when you are young, when you are in the care of your parents. You start looking around at others and deciding what you want to be. Then you consider what the costs are. Then you evaluate the cost versus the benefit. Then you conclude whether you are willing to pay the price to achieve the results. So as you grow and mature and watch the people in your environment, you make decisions as to who you want to be."

"Wait a minute. You don't decide who you want to be. You decide what you can do and what you can't do," I interrupt.

"That is not true. Look at all the athletes you see in sports today. There are plenty of people performing at levels that nobody thought were possible."

"They are the exceptions."

"What makes an exception, idiot? Someone who, when evaluating the cost versus the results, decided the results would be worth it. You gotta have faith, moron."

"Sure, faith is enough!"

> Mark 12:22–23. In *reply Jesus said to the disciples, "If you only have faith in God—this is the absolute truth—you can say to this Mount of Olives, 'Rise up and fall into the Mediterranean,' and your command will he obeyed. All that's required is that you really believe and have no doubt!'*

"What do you think Jesus meant when He said that? No one, including the disciples, has sent the Mount of Olives into the Mediterranean. Maybe what He was trying to tell you was through faith in God, you can do anything. So now we are back to, 'What do you really want to do?' Some will say, 'I don't want to practice every day. I don't want to wear that sweaty uniform and get the poo knocked out of me for old glory.' That's okay, but that's a choice. So you looked at the sweat, odor, and pain; weigh your potential; and chose not to go that route. Life is filled with choices."

"So you are saying that if I was a loser, it's because I chose to be one!"

"That's right, little Pervert. Don't that stink! Who do you blame? Where can you go with that? Well, you can go to hell." He laughs loudly.

"Very funny, Eluder. Somehow I don't see the humor."

"Here is the deal, bad boy. The one thing heaven and hell have in common is there are no excuses accepted in either place. You made choices all of your days on earth. Everyone is given opportunities to find God. You must choose to look for Him. Here is the evaluation process. If I go with God, my friends will ridicule me, and I will have to give up this lifestyle. Now comes the decision. Is the cost worth the results? The choice is yours. You made it and you alone will pay the piper. When you go before Jesus, there won't be anyone standing there beside you. There won't be any counsel to represent you. The gate to heaven is narrow. Only one at a time can pass through. There is no one to blame. You stand alone for every good deed and every evil deed you performed. There will be no intersession. Your whole life will pass before you. There will be no hiding anything. You will be judged according to how you lived your life. Jesus was willing to be the intercessor while you were on the earth. Even though you made all those wrong choices, you still had the opportunity to change. All you had to do was choose that option. Now, for you, the time has come to view the scales. Guilty or innocent? This is where the politically correct wet their pants. There is no counsel, no attorney to represent you, no therapist to explain how you were mistreated. Your life is your defense. Guilty or innocent?"

"So walk with Jesus or burn in hell?"

"You got it."

"That is just so unacceptable! I can't imagine a God who is loving and yet that black and white. That cold. Did God appear before me, and say, 'I am God almighty'? Did He say, 'You have only one chance to get to heaven and that is to follow my son Jesus'? Did He say to me, 'You must choose between heaven and hell'? No! I was right there every day. No one spoke to me. No one said, I am God and you need to change the way you are living'."

"Well, there you have it. Not guilty! So what if when you went to church, you thought the preacher couldn't make the top ten best-dressed list. So you put him down and mocked him, the person who was trying to tell you the very things you are raving about."

"That's a good point. I admit there were opportunities. However, something as important as this, one would think God would have given me a lot more opportunities."

"Remember the girl? The real pretty one who lived in the same apartment complex when you were with the insurance company?"

"Yeah. So?"

"So remember saying to yourself she was the prettiest girl you had ever seen up close? Remember how impressed you were with her beauty and sweet disposition? You thought at the time, 'Man, what I wouldn't give to get a girl like that'."

"So what's your point?"

"You smiled at her so much you thought your face was going to fall off. Then came the payoff. She asked you out."

"Wait a minute, wait a minute, Eluder! You have finally become delusional! She never asked me out."

"Remember on that Friday? You told the guys you would meet them at the bar down the street. They said that girl from work who slept with two of the guys you work with would be there. Do you remember, she was the one who every time she and her boyfriend fell out, she would go out and tie one on and end up waking up at some guys house?"

"I remember, I remember."

"As you were going in to your apartment after work, in a hurry to get cleaned up and get to the bar, your neighbor approached you. She asked if you were busy that night. You were floored. You said, 'What do you have in mind?' She said with a beautiful smile, 'I'm going to church tonight to hear this guy who is really wonderful, and I would love it if you would go with me.' You said no. You, who had earlier said to yourself, if only I had the chance to go out with her, man, that would be the ultimate."

"That wasn't an invitation for a date. It was an offer to go to church."

"She considered it the same thing. She was asking you out in the hopes you shared some of the same interest. Then you left and went to the bar. Guess what? Loser lucked out! The office favorite got so drunk she went home with you. Threw up in your bed, too. Remember what she looked like that Saturday morning? She was ticked. She said you got her so drunk, it made her sick. Kind of hard to make it with a girl who just threw up, but you managed. So the next Monday at work all the guys gave you the high five. Mr. Cool. Yeah, you got your turn. However, that Saturday morning when you were trying to get that pitiful-looking thing to her car without anybody noticing—is God good or what? Just as soon as you opened the door and moved out, the one vulnerable spot, there she stood, the girl who invited you to church. Remember how beautiful she looked? Remember how embarrassed you were when she realized what was going on? God rescues His children from dogs like you, Pervert. It seems she never spoke to you again. Didn't you happen to notice how the girls at the office started avoiding you? Of course you did, that's why you changed jobs. Wonder what the drunk said about you?"

"Man....You are a real jerk. You just love to find the fly in the ointment."

"That wasn't ointment, it was vomit. And it wasn't a fly, it was you. Choices, choices. If only you would have made a few choices that required some character. If you would have gone to church with your neighbor, she would have turned your whole life around. But that required some character to make a choice like that."

"Remember that time in school when those guys were beating up on the little nerd? You wanted to help, and you almost did. Then you looked over and some of the cool guys in the school were laughing. Hey, you knew you would be uncool if you stepped in."

"Yeah, plus I would have been beaten to death by the jerks."

"That's not true. You weren't afraid of the boys beating him up, it was the guys watching. Guess what? The guy, Trey, who you always thought was so cool, if you would have jumped in, he would have followed. You would have started a friendship that would have lasted the rest of your life....Choices."

"You know, the reason I made such bad choices is because of my childhood. I was never given the guidance others were."

"Oh, my goodness. Open the doors. There has been a terrible mistake. The Pervert was sent here unjustly. Somebody! Over here!"

"Hey, get off of it! Do you think it was easy growing up as me?"

"Yes."

"Well, that shows what you know. I was never shown the love my friends got at home. My father left when I was only eight years old. People were constantly asking me where my father was. When I was young, I would make up stories about how he worked with the CIA and was never home. Then as I got older, I would tell them my father died in a plane crash."

"So now what, titty baby? Do we break out the violins? Poor little Pervert. Nobody loved him. His daddy ran off and he was all alone."

"What kind of sadistic jerk are you?"

"There are people without arms, legs, and parents who made it to heaven, Pervert. I'm sorry. There is no free ride. The only thing free was the blood of Jesus. He spilled His blood for you, and it was free to you. That's it. There is no more. You either accepted it or you didn't. Your whiny little story makes no difference. People who were persecuted have a story. You, Pervert, have no story. All you had was opportunity."

"How can you say that? How can you make it look as though all I had to do was make the right choice?" I argue.

"Because that is all that was required. Don't feel alone. Most of the people on your planet will be joining you and me. To say that God didn't make it easy enough for you just doesn't stand up. The reward is great. The opportunity to spend all eternity in heaven, where the streets are paved with gold, is enough. What more could a God offer someone as an incentive? 'Follow my Son and live forever in heaven, or rebel, and spend eternity in hell.' Let's see. Eternity in heaven or eternity in hell. Now, from where we are standing I would say the choice is clear. Weak people make bad decisions. One must have the character to resist the world, to embrace the Son of God and His word, to pick up their sword and follow Jesus."

"Something is really wrong with this picture."

"Yes. I'm sure to you it looks distorted. Nevertheless, God didn't make you to judge Him. He made you to be judged. Somehow, in past generations, your family chose to no longer honor God. Instead, they chose to consider themselves above the law. Now it is judgment day, and you are wailing. On earth you can ride above the law for a while. But here in eternity there are no people with that illustriousness. I truly feel your pain, Pervert. It is obvious that you feel above the law. You feel you should be given consideration. This is not just about you. I know your mommy told you everything was about you, but guess what? She was wrong. You know that man she married? Well, with him came the sins of his father and his father's father. So your mother had choices to make, too. When your grandfather and grandmother courted, they got to know each other's family. There was a reason. Your family screams out who you are. So if a woman doesn't have good decision-making skills and has broken her relationship with her family, then she is responsible for the choices she makes. Her children will pay for the choices she makes. If she chooses to sleep with a man before she is married or to many a man without knowing him and his family as well as she should, then there is a price to pay. You can't have it both ways. You can't say to the judge, 'Your Honor, I didn't know she was that kind of person.' The judge will say to you, 'Then your crime is not spending the time necessary to make the proper evaluation'."

"Well, in a perfect world…."

"The world is perfect," the Eluder snarls.

"Well, if the world is a perfect place, then why does this place exist?"

"In a perfect world there is a heaven and a hell. There is up as well as down. There is sin and there is righteousness. There is perfect judgment with a reward and punishment. There is good and evil. In a perfect world the righteous will praise God and the evil will curse Him. Everything is perfect, Pervert. You are where you are supposed to be. That is purity to a flawlessness that man cannot understand. There must be evil for good to exist. There can't be a reward unless there is a punishment. There can't be eternal jubilation without eternal sorrow. What good is a celebration if there is no victory?"

"Victory over what?"

"Who has ever heard of being victorious over nothing? What's the point? Why bother? If victory is over an unworthy opponent, then there is no true victory. Conclusion: Victory must be over a deserving adversary. The stakes are extreme. The challenge is absolute. There is no middle ground. You prevail or you fall."

"Why wasn't I told this? No, really, why didn't they teach this in school? Why didn't my mother explain this to me as I was growing up? What kind of justice is this?"

"We are back to the choices your family made through the years. Your grandfather was a womanizer. He liked to chase the girls. His father, a man of God, told him about God. His father brought him up in a church, but when your grandfather was old enough, he left home and started on a path of rebellion. He quit going to church. He started sleeping with prostitutes and different women he worked with. Your father saw how he lived. Your grandfather didn't take your father to church, so your father had no solid foundation. Your father admired your grandfather. He wanted to be like him. So he chased the girls, too. Your mother came from a broken home and had no father to insist she go to church with her mother. The reason your grandmother went to church was the desire to find a husband. Your mother was appalled and felt your grandmother was a hypocrite. So your mother decided she would find a man outside of church. She felt it was a more honest approach. The problem was what she found was your father, who just wanted to have sex. He wasn't looking for a wife. He knew if he went home with a wife who was pregnant, your grandfather would mock him. So your father moved away. So let's recap. Your grandfather, father, and father-in-law are all present and accounted for."

"You mean…."

'Yes, three generations are right here."

"How can that be?"

"Easy. Your grandfather rebelled. He knew better, but wanted his own way. Your great-grandfather begged him to come back home and to go back to church, but your grandfather refused to listen. Your grandfather knew God's word, but chose to rebel. Now comes the three-generation curse. Your father never went to church. Oh, he walked through the door on occasion, for the wedding of a friend or a funeral. He never went to church to see what God was all about. Why? Because of his father's sin. His rebellious father denied him the opportunity to know the Lord. So your father didn't even feel obliged to stick around when he heard about you. Your father had no one in his life to direct him to the Lord. So he continued to make bad choices. You might say, then, how can anyone escape that web? Through God all things are possible. Your father sat up one night drinking heavy. He was fighting with the idea of marriage to your mother. Every time he would start to consider what it might be like married to your mother, he would think of the ridicule of your grandfather laughing at him and telling him he married a whore. He just couldn't take the scorn. You see, Pervert, it takes a lot of courage to do the right thing. The people in heaven belong in heaven. You and I belong here."

"You're right. We do belong here. I think I'm starting to get it. There is a price to pay for everything. There are no free rides. I guess I thought that as long as I was doing what I wanted to do and I wasn't hurting anyone, that it was okay. I felt I was entitled to do my own thing, to be selfish. I think I even heard some TV shrink say that was okay."

"You're right. The TV shrinks tell you to look after number one and everything will be all right. They say if you're happy, then the people around you will be happy for you. That's bull."

"I see that now. If only I had thought of someone other than myself. I don't think I had one thought that wasn't about me. Oh, God, what a jerk I was! What a loser! The only time I ever did anything for someone else was when I was looking for praise, someone to tell me what a wonderful person I was," I lament.

"Now you are starting to enter the period called 'The Verified Era'. This is a time of great sorrowfulness. You will not be required to participate in any of the functions until you have completed this phase. Now the Governor AMBRIOL, he who continuously comforts, will stay with you through this stage. When you are available, you will be returned to me." The Eluder fades away.

AMBRIOL appears and says. "Come with me."

"Sure. Where are we going?" I ask.

"Does it matter?"

"Well, I guess not."

"There are many things for you to think about."

"I feel like the dumbest guy ever born. How could I be so stupid? What do I do?"

"The main thing is you must do is accept your fate. Realize that you are where you are supposed to be. Once you accept that, things get easier," AMBRIOL offers.

"Do you think that if my grandfather knew what was going to happen, he would have sent all of us to hell?"

"Of course not. Your grandfather is no different than you. He felt that God was something the goodie-two-shoes made up so they could have everyone under control. So he just wanted to have a good time. What's so terrible about that? He knew his father wouldn't understand. He was never able to talk to his father. His father always had to read scripture to him. All he wanted to do was talk to his dad. His father was afraid. He could see the spark in your grandfather's eyes. He was constantly trying to read the word to your grandfather, but it would have a reverse effect. Your grandfather just had to see what was on the other side. He couldn't contain himself.

Once he went over to the other side, he couldn't come back. Oh, the sweet taste of a woman, the wonderful feeling you get when you're high! Your grandfather was a nice-looking man. The women loved him. He could name the game, and they would play. Periodically he would think of his father, but his pride would never let him go back. The people your grandfather hung around were always telling him how great he was, how much the girls liked him, how much the men admired him. To humble himself and go see his father was more than he could stand. When he talked of his life, everybody bragged on him. If he told his father about his life, he would have to hang his head in shame."

"So we were sold down the drain for a measure of pride?"

"Well, know this. Pride is our number one seduction. There is no greater temptation. The reason pride is number one on God's hate list is because of its grasp on humans. They have so much trouble escaping the clutches of pride. Pride is power. When you are prideful, you feel as though you are in charge. You think things are going to go your way. A prideful person says things like, 'If it's to be, it's up to me,' or 'I'm a take-charge person'. It's very difficult to build up your self-esteem and feel as though you are in charge, only to have someone tell you that without God, you are nothing. You are insignificant. This is what the Christian teaching is about. They tell you, you are nothing. Only God is important. Well? When you've been told all your life that you are important, it gets hard to swallow the 'you're nothing' pill."

"So what does that mean?"

"it means your grandfather made some bad choices, just like everybody else who's here. That doesn't mean he was a terrible guy. It just means the mistakes he made were big ones, the ones that cost you your eternal soul."

"What a jerk! I hope he has to pay for all the suffering he has caused us."

"Let's see."

The same hologram opens up. There are all these people moaning and screaming, calling out to someone to help them.

"Do you see the ones buried to the waist?"

"Yes."

"The one holding himself with both hands is your grandfather."

"What kind of slop are they in?"

"Mud. It's mud. The worms live well in the mud. That's why it's there. During his life your grandfather's gift was his good looks and body. Now, to negate his gifts, he has been placed in the pit of the repulsive. When he was on earth, people admired him. Now they are disgusted when they see him. And look, look. Right next to him is your father! The one trying to pick the worms out of his skin."

"Okay. Enough!"

"Sorry, Pervert. I thought you wanted to see their punishment."

"I just thought I did. Another bad choice on my part."

It is obvious we are changing rooms. This room is a rugged but somehow beautiful room. Like the other, the opening is very large. The inside is almost Egyptian. It has all these magnificent chairs. They look like something from a king's palace.

"Go ahead, have a seat. Sit anywhere you would like."

"Wow, this is awesome. You know, if my grandfather would have continued on the path his father made for him, well, there would have been a chance my father would have continued on that path."

"That is very likely. Your father was easily impressed. Anything your grandfather did, your dad wanted to do."

"So my grandfather is the reason we are all here," I utter.

"No. Your grandfather is the reason your grandfather is here. Your father is the reason your father is here, and you are the reason you are here."

"But if my grandfather had walked with the Lord, then things might have been different."

"I'm sure it would be consoling to allow your grandfather to take full responsibility for all the decisions you and your father made. But the truth demands justice, and justice says every man must stand and be judged. There can be no alternative. The one who lived the life must be the one judged. Believe it or not, you were in charge of you. There was no one else at the helm. Sorry."

"I know, I know, I think that was just one last attempt to pass the buck. What the hell, I guess I am where I should be."

"Everybody is. There is no other way. In a perfect universe all actions demand consequences. You didn't finish college, but I'm sure you have heard someone say for every action there is an equal and opposite reaction?"

"Yes."

"Well, this is a law. The laws exist throughout the universe. The Creator of the universe put these laws into effect. Once they are enacted, there can be no changing them, not until the Creator comes back and declares the end of the age. At that precise instant in time, the present era will end, and the laws that govern it will terminate."

"Then what? I mean, like, what will the earth and universe be like then?"

"There will no longer be a sun. The earth will no longer have these laws to endure. The earth and heaven will be as one. God will live on the earth along with His people. This is why there will be no sun. There won't be any need for it. God emits light and is the total source of all life."

"So the people who are saved will work under the supervision of the angels as they do here?"

"No. The people who make it to heaven will be above the angels."

"Then why do some people on earth worship angels?"

"Out of ignorance. If they had read the Bible, they would have discovered that every time man tried to bow to an angel, he was told not to bow. This is because angels are angelic beings, made to serve God and man."

"That's a switch."

"For those who were humble on earth and were willing to let the loud and proud rule, this will be their age. They will be comforted. This will be their time for serenity."

Just now there's a mighty crash! There are eight beings who somehow have broken through the barrier and are now in our area. It appears four of the beings are together and are considering confronting the other four. As they rise, I'm thinking I must be in harm's way. They are walking around the area, as a wrestler does before jumping his opponent. Now, just moments later, they are in an all-out war. Initially, they looked like winged muscle men with ugly faces. But as they start fighting, it's vicious. Their hands can somehow accommodate talons, and their teeth are like those of a baboon. They are slashing each other and jumping on the other's backs and ripping each other open with their teeth. It is so vicious. I must turn away.

LAPARIN suddenly appears.

The beings aren't paying any attention to him. He holds up his hand, and the beings start screaming.

LAPARIN says, "You Kerubic Angels are in a restricted area. Leave at once."

The Kerubic Angels flee the area immediately but are still looking intently at each other. I can only assume this will continue somewhere else.

LAPARIN looks really ticked. I am so scared, I think I might wet my pants. I'm not sure why I didn't. I don't know if it's the new body or some other reason. All I know is you have to see it to believe it.

"Boy, good thing LAPARIN is over the Kerubic Angels!" I whisper.

"It was a good thing he appeared. However, he is not over the Kerubic Angels. They are above the Aries and Governors."

"Then how did he overtake them?"

"The power he used was that of the Dark Angel who sent him. He is responsible for you until you have become an Eluder. So when you were in harm's way, the Dark Angel who healed you before sent LAPARIN. When he held his hand up, he was asking for the Dark Angel to intervene.

"That's twice the Dark Angel has saved my life."

"Yes, this is true. The Dark Angel likes you. He knows all there is to know about you and has compassion for you. You must rest now. Once you have had sufficient rest, you may begin with your disciplining," AMBRIOL says quietly.

"What does that entail?"

"You must learn the true teachings of the Bible so you won't get tripped up when you are in a battle."

"That's how the Eluder knew so much about the Bible."

"Yes. You are right. All of our Eluders must take this curriculum so they won't be trapped by the Holy Ghost."

"May I ask a question?"

"Yes," AMBRIOL replies.

"Why were the Kerubic Angels fighting?"

"Kerubic Angels are warriors. They will be among the first when the end of times come. They will be on the front line. Their fighting is encouraged in the proper areas. The Dark Angel knew you were frightened, so he halted the skirmish. Some of our Eluders love to see the Kerubic Angels fight. They look at it as sport. They are beautiful specimens and are perfect for engaging in combat."

"Do they only attack each other?"

"The Angels from different Kerubim fight one another for practice. They are summoned, from time to time, to go with the Dark Angels when there is an angelic war going on.

"They have been known to ambush VSNARDA, though he is more than twice their size. The Kerubic Angels are fierce warriors. They have no fear of destruction. It is said that Satan loves to see them fight to the death. Then one of the Dark Angels will bring them back to life. VSNARDA can kill a Kerubic Angel quite easily. So what they do is send one straight ahead to get the attention of VSNARDA. Then, as he attacks the Kerubic Angel, the other three come in from the back. They can inflict a great deal of damage before they are slain."

"So there are only four Kerubic Angels?"

"No, there are sixteen. There are RZLA, TAAD, BOZA, DOPA , each having three companions."

"Why don't they travel together?"

"Because they hate each other. Remember when you were in the bar?"

"Yeah… There were eight Kerubic Angels, and it was getting ugly."

"You are lucky you didn't have to stick around and see the finish. When you have two groups of warriors in the same area, you will usually have hostility."

"Will LAPARIN punish them or the Dark Angel?"

"Neither. They are under the rule of their Archangel."

"Who is their Archangel?"

"You witnessed TAAD and his companions AADT, ADTA and DTAA, of Water, fighting BOZA and companions OZAB, ZABO and ABOZ, of Earth. The ruler of Water is ETAAD, and the ruler of Earth is ABOZA. These two Archangels will determine if there is any punishment for the Kerubic Angels."

"Are the Archangels as large and as vicious as VSNARDA?"

AMBRIOL chuckles. "The Archangels are beautiful. They look like angels from heaven.

"When the Archangels are in the presence of the Kerubic Angels, the Kerubics act like little children sitting on the floor, nice and docile. Not even a peep. The Archangels, Dark Angels, and Satan all came from heaven. They formed an alliance to help Satan conquer the throne. Now, rest and soon you will learn the Truth."

Time passes. Oh, man, it seems as though I have been sleeping forever. I guess it's time to learn the Truth. Suddenly there is a being present.

"My name is LIIANSA, one of the Seniors, and referred to as he who is first in truth."

"So what's next?" I ask.

"You must learn the word of God," LIIANSA answers.

"Why would I come to hell to learn the word of God? I had plenty of chances to do that on earth."

"Of course you did. Now you are going to learn it so you can be an effective Eluder."

"Why does an Eluder need to know the word of God?"

"If you don't know the Truth, then you can't fight it. The Truth is our enemy. How could you possibly fight an enemy you don't know? Idiots don't win battles. That's why not everyone can be an Eluder. Just as in anything you have ever done in your life on earth, if you succeeded, you had to know what you were doing. It is no different here."

"What I don't get is why the Bible is so important."

"Okay, I'm going to explain this only once. If you don't get it, then you don't qualify to be an Eluder, and I'll kick you out, so listen carefully. If you don't know your enemy, you can't defeat him. No one goes to war without first preparing for a fight. How many men do they have? What kinds of weapons are available to them? Who are their leaders? What kind of experience do their leaders have?"

"Okay, okay, got the picture."

"If you are going to help us recruit, you must be convincing. If you are constantly overcome with the Truth and you don't know how to combat it, how can you be effective?"

"So I have to know what the Truth is, so I can distort it," I ask.

"Yes."

"Do most of the people know the Truth?"

"No. The real beauty of free will is God gave these imbeciles the freedom to choose, and they misuse it."

"Man, we have become such jerks."

'Look, this isn't anything new. This has been going on ever since God gave man the freedom. That's why we had the great flood. God, even back then, was so fed up with the way mankind exploited his freedom of choice that He all but wiped them out—exterminated almost the entire species.

"What did He do?"

"You are slow! I thought everybody new about Noah and the ark?"

"I've heard about Noah and the ark. I thought you were talking about something else. Was that a true story?"

"Everything in the Bible is true."

"So God really destroyed everything on the earth?"

"Yes. After the flood, God looked at the earth and felt great sorrow. He said he would never do that again. He created the rainbow as a sign to remind man of His promise. So even though there have been many generations that deserve to be wiped off the face of the earth, God made a promise never to do that again."

"Okay. You said most of the people don't know the truth."

"That's right. So when we tell them something wrong, they don't know the difference. They are either too lazy to look it up or too stupid. Who cares why? It's just how it is. Man is too arrogant to ask someone."

"Why do you say that?"

"Let's look at the first lie ever told on the earth. The original lie. Our lord told this one himself, and it is a perfect example of how to distort the truth."

"What was the first lie?"

"Our lord (Satan) appeared in the Garden of Eden as a serpent. Listen to the master of lies and learn the art of deception. The first thing Satan told the woman was in Genesis 3:1–5: '*Really?' he asked 'None of the fruit in the garden? God* says *you mustn't eat any of it?'* The first thing you must do when looking to deceive is diversion. Satan has already created diversion when he asked a question, and in the original question was a lie." He laughs. "Beautiful.... So the woman is on the offense, because she is righteous. '*Of course we may eat it,' the woman told him. 'It's only the fruit from the tree at the center of the garden that we are not to eat. God* says *we mustn't eat it or even touch it, or we will die.'* Is our lord Satan great or what? He told a lie with a little truth in it. The woman was made to feel as though she corrected him. This starts the old ego. Then he turns her pride on her, by telling her God has made a fool of her. *'That's a lie!' the serpent hissed. 'You'll not die! God knows very well that the instant you eat it you will become like him, for your eyes will he opened—you will be able to distinguish good from evil!'* you see how she fell right in the trap? It is the same trap we are using today. Do you think they have learned? They still fall for it. All you have to do is tap that ego, and the odds are in your favor."

"You mean people are still falling for the same thing?"

"Oh, yes. The exact same one. That is why pride is number one on God's hit list, it's the one Satan used to start the downfall of man. Look at America. What do you think most Americans would say if you told them you thought they were inadequate in something they felt secure in? Do you suppose they would humbly solicit your assistance?"

"I think they would string you up."

"Proverbs 16:18: *Pride goes before destruction and haughtiness before a fall.* Proverbs 8:13: *If anyone respects and fears God, he will hate evil. For wisdom hates pride, arrogance, corruption and deceit of every kind."*

"I thought having pride was a good thing. I thought all the people who are rich and famous have big egos and lots of pride."

"Do you think lots of the rich and famous are in heaven?"

"Well, maybe not."

"I think you're starting to get it. Through the years there have been some people who have made a lot of money and had fame but were able to continue with a humble spirit."

"Yeah. Give me one movie star that is in heaven, and I'll move on."

"Roy Rogers, king of the cowboys, and in his day, a big star."

"Okay. Do most of the TV evangelists make it to heaven?"

"You would be surprised. Most of them have a lot of success. You see, we love to see the pastor have a large congregation. We love to see him go on TV and grow to a national level. Then guess what happens? There is an enormous business to run. There isn't time to think about poor old Ms. Jones. Why, the pastor has four meetings to attend today. He has a staff to instruct. He needs to go to the board meeting to assure himself the money is being invested properly. If he doesn't agree with what the main body of the church is saying, he may pull away and start his own church. We have provided so many distractions that if a pastor has what it takes to bring people to the Lord, we pour it on him. Then when he starts to have success, we overwhelm him. Think about it. Who would want to go back to a small church once they have filled the house? Man, what a feeling that must be! Some have told us it's equal to that of a rock star. To come up on a stage and have hundreds, in some cases thousands, of people watching you. Some of the TV evangelists have millions watching them. Now, what better thing to have someone entangled in? Do you think once you reach a certain level that if things start to go a little south, people won't try anything to save the ship? Believe me, there have been some good men who started in the ministry and had great success and one day look around and realized they were surrounded by sharks. Most of the time it was too late. They couldn't admit they were in over their head. That's right! The old pride got them, the loyalty to the people following them. They couldn't stop the show because of all the people counting on them.

"The best thing we have going for us is success! The greatest weapon we have is success. These poor ministers think they are judged by the size of their congregation. The opposite is true. They forgot to look at their examples. Paul, the great evangelist, worked as a tent maker to pay his way. He wouldn't take money from the churches he visited so no one could look on him as greedy. He took beatings from governments and abuse from all sorts of adversaries. So when the people of today look at Paul's counterparts, they find Armadi suits and Mercedes Benzes. These are the very people Paul said to beware of. Hey, life is good. All we have to do is give them what they want. Success!" He howls.

"They drowned in their own desires."

"What about Billy Graham?"

"Wow! You found one man."

"What about Mother Theresa?"

"That's two."

"Those are the only ones I know."

"Those are the exceptions, not the rule. Do you think most of the pastors suffered as Mother Theresa? Do you think most of the evangelists are as honest as Billy Graham? Let's see, how many men of the cloth do you think there are in your country? How many do you think live the life of the two you just mentioned?"

"Probably only a handful. So does that mean all the rest are coming here?"

"God's word says they will be judged on a higher level than the others. So when they stand before God, they will stand as someone who professed to know God. They will be judged for the way they lived their lives, as leaders of God's people. Believe me, that is a level they will wish they had never asked for, if they are not sincere. Thieves and perverts are better off than those who falsely claim to be men of God. All the riches they enjoy on the earth won't help them when they come here."

"What punishment do they receive?"

"They are next to Judas Iscariot."

"Who is that?"

"He is the man who betrayed Jesus! He was one of the twelve disciples. He betrayed Jesus to His enemies for thirty silver coins."

"No way! He sold Jesus out for thirty silver coins? How stupid was this guy?"

"As they say in the world you just left. 'He's toast'."

"LIIANSA, answer this. What's the big deal about sex?" I ask.

'That is a good question. The problem with sex is it was meant for Adam and Eve. Sex was to be a thing of joy. But once the world was corrupted, everything changed."

"So why is everyone I know so caught up in sex?"

"It's one of our favorite things. Sex is connected to rebellion. If someone has a rebellious heart, one of the easiest ways to find out is through sex."

"I don't get it."

"Everybody in the free world knows sex before marriage is wrong. Right?"

"Right."

"So why is it so prevalent? Because someone with a rebellious heart is looking for some reason to rebel. They don't want to look stupid, but their rebellious heart won't be satisfied until they have revolted. So the most exploitable possibility for us is sex. Most people who rebel against God have this in common. They are sexually active. In the eyes of God, outside of marriage, this is unacceptable. There is no gray area. This is black and white."

"Why is it connected to rebellion? I don't see what sex has to do with rebellion."

"I understand. You have to look past the act of sex. Here is an example. A man is married to a pretty woman, who is faithful to him. Someone saw him in a bar with a girl that was by most standards plain. Why do you think the man was with the ugly girl when he has a pretty wife who loves him at home?"

"Because he likes sex! Yeah, baby!"

"Wrong! That doesn't make any sense. Think about it. Don't just blurt out something superficial like the idiot you were on earth. Think. Why wouldn't this man be with his wife? She is pretty, she knows what he likes, and she wants to be with him."

"It's the challenge!"

"What challenge? What did the man win?"

"He got laid!"

"By a lesser woman than his wife. His wife is a woman of principle, so, as to a challenge, the person sleeping with his wife would be declared the winner. He spent money that belonged to his family on a woman who doesn't care if he lives or dies. The one night could cost him his health, his marriage, and his soul. So what was gained?"

"Man, you are making it sound as though he is stupid. The guys who worked with me and hung out where I did were considered cool if they could pick up the chicks."

"You were a rebel. You hung out with other rebels."

"Why are you calling us rebels? We were just regular guys."

"Rebels are people who can't live by the laws of the land. God gave the first laws.

Everyone who rejects them is a rebel."

"Okay. Now I get it. I was a rebel. Using that ruler, I was a rebel."

"That is the only ruler. So when you use God's word as law, everyone who rejects His word is a rebel. There are so many people with a rebellious heart, our job is easy. We just need to provide them with opportunity. These poor slobs are just as you were. They think they are out there being cool. They want people to look at them. They want to be noticed the exact opposite of what God's word teaches. His word says to be meek, have a humble heart. Our guys say, 'Look at me. I can drink more, sleep with more women, and do all the other things that go with rebelling'. You see, the guy hiding in the bushes waiting to rob you is no more a rebel than the guy looking at your wife, plotting how he can win her affections."

"Both are the same?"

"Both are rebelling against God's word. Both refuse to humble themselves and follow Him. They must have their own way. This is the mark of a rebel. Do you think everyone of these people like to wake up with pounding headaches? Do you think they like looking in the mirror the next morning, knowing their spouses don't know what liars and cheats they are? Do you think these people are having a wonderful time?"

"Of course they are! The next morning is just the price they have to pay."

"Is that right? Well, remember the little blonde you lost the job over? The one everybody at work said was so good looking? All the guys said they would give up their job for a night with that. Remember?"

"Yeah. She was one good-looking woman."

"The truth is you had a bad night. The two of you were very awkward. You were both very drunk. You both slept late. You were fired. You never actually had sex with her. Don't you remember? Surely you don't call that sex."

"Okay, okay, it was a bad night."

"You lost a job over trying to be cool, over the opportunity to sleep with someone you thought would enhance your reputation. Look at the logic. What did you really gain? The decent people in the office all thought you were a loser. Only the rebels were impressed. You see, from a sexual view point, it was a terrible experience."

"You're right."

"It truly had nothing to do with sex. It had everything to do with rebellion. That's what makes us so good. We know what is behind the mind. I love it. The truth is people who want to have really good sex will have it with their spouse. People who want to rebel will have sex with someone other than a spouse. This can be a life mate, roommate, acquaintance, anyone other than what God's word says is acceptable."

"Do you realize how many people fall into that category?"

"Yes. That's why the road to hell is wide enough for the multitudes, and the road the heaven is less traveled."

"I think I'm starting to get it. Sex is just an alternate journey for a rebel running from God's word."

"Ah, you're arriving. The point is, sex isn't as great as they say it is anyway. It's the hunt. How many times have you heard them refer to it as the hunt? To the girls as the trophy? It's all about rebellion. Having your own way. Not God's way, but your way. That is a losing proposition."

"So once a child has a rebellious heart, does that mean there is no hope for him?"

"No, it just means there is going to be a rough road ahead. One can be beaten down so that they will finally surrender. This is something we don't want to do. We want them to have their own way. People were made in God's image. This means they will always have a pulling inside. Their soul was designed to follow God, but with the perversion of sin, that has all changed. Now, the soul is quietly crying out. Even the worst of criminals have the pulling going on inside. They just shut it out. Some can't take it and drop to their knees and ask for forgiveness. They can't take the torment of constantly going against what they know is right."

"So we all know right from wrong. Refusing to do what is right is rebelling?" I mutter.

"Refusing to follow God is renouncing. There will always be those who think they know what is right. The only way to walk with God is to follow Him. The only way to God is through Jesus. It is obvious that Jesus paid a profound price. Those who can humble themselves to God, the ones who can call out to God, using Jesus' name, will be heard. Those who are too proud to humble themselves and continue to rebel will share this wonderful life with us for all eternity. We are the compelling forces, being today's 'Logic'. You see, if we can keep the people proud enough to feel like what they think can compare to God's word, we are moving them in our direction. A young man ponders sex with his girlfriend. His father isn't a Christian. Therefore, his father gives him logic-inspired advice. Upon hearing his father's advice about responsibility, the young man comes to the conclusion that it's okay to have responsible sex. If the girl's parents aren't Christians, she will be told about responsible sex. She will be given to logic. So there is no fear of God. The young individuals are left to their own reason.

"People don't tell their daughters it's okay to have sex!"

"When you tell them their body is theirs to protect and to do with as they choose, they assume you mean they make the choices of when, where, and who, all by themselves. There is never any mention of God or His laws. There's no thought as to committing a sin against God. They are merely trying to determine, through logic, which scenario is best for them."

"Why is logic such a bad way to develop?"

"It's the rebel's way. The rebel must have his own way. Logic is just an extension of his insolence. You see, when you use logic, you leave God out. You say to yourself, 'What makes me feel good or 'What do I feel like the outcome should be?' This has nothing to do with reading God's word and humbling yourself and submitting yourself to God's word. Logic is based on one's own ego. I know what is best for me, based on my experiences. Trust me, modern man's wisdom has nothing to do with God. That makes us very happy."

"Would you give me an example?"

"Logic 101. You can find the answer to one of life's problems. You go to a counselor. This person is not a Christian counselor. What can they do for you? If they don't know God and His laws, all they can do is listen and hope you come up with the answer yourself. Now, if they are truly arrogant, they might try and fix you using some Dr. Feelgood's hypothesis. Boy, then you are really in trouble."

"Is there a way to tell if someone is on the right track?" I ask.

"The litmus test is rudimentary. There is only one question: Is the information you are receiving God-based? If it is based on God's word, then everything is based on the truth. God's word will always keep a man on the pathway of righteousness. It will keep him out of harm's way. If it is based on anything other than God's word, the door is open for us to come in. All we need is someone to think too highly of himself. Then comes the cogitating and using one's own intellectual prowess: discovery, followed by conclusion, followed by judgment. Once judgment is complete, one accepts it as reality. One's own reality is perceived as truth. Now look what we have. I think, therefore it is. A cesspool at best! Just think about it. What poetic justice! A man's ego is the distribution center for his soul. His ego determines his post in eternity. God's formula is E+R=D. Ego + Rebellion = Death. H+C=L. Humility ± Christ = Life. If a man thinks more highly of himself than he should, he can't humble himself. He wants to be in the light, but he can't see the light with his head bowed. So a person with a considerable ego must go his own way. This is called rebellion even though he doesn't intend it to be. When you have your own way, you are choosing to be a nonconformist. You can't have your cake and eat it too. You either submit to God or have your own way. Our lord (Satan) can attest there are no rebels in heaven.

"So the correct thing to tell the daughter is to follow God's word. The father should interview the boy. If he doesn't seem like an honorable boy, the father should not allow his daughter to date the boy. Most of your modern-day fathers don't have the backbone to stand up and tell everyone concerned, no one can date his daughter without his consent. To date a boy is getting to know him as the only purpose. Once she gets to know him, she will know his heart."

"If he is not a humble man, with God in his heart, you must end the relationship?"

"Precisely."

'Now, if I understand you, sex is all just a lure. Other than for reproduction and marital privilege, sex is irrelevant. It's a distraction. Taking one's eye offthe road. Allowing him to lose direction."

"Excellent. You are starting to get it. You see, sex is modern man's apple. Now we don't have an apple, but we do have sex. So God said not to eat the apple. The rebel in them went for the apple. God says not to have sex until you are married. The rebel in them makes them crazy with anticipation. Do you remember before you had sex how you used to think about it all the time? How it consumed you?"

"Yes, yes!"

"When you finally had sex, was it everything you hoped it would be?"

"No. Not even close."

"But you didn't tell the other guys that it wasn't that great?"

"No."

"We figured that out, too. You see, once a person has sinned, they do the same thing Eve did. They drag someone else down with them. Once you have violated your body, there is a certain sadness. You don't know what it is. You just know it's sad. Usually people don't realize it's because they have broken one of God's laws. They just know they don't feel real good about themselves. So what do they do? They do what any respectable rebel does. They rationalize. They justify. 'Come on in. The water is fine.' How many kids do you think are telling other kids, 'I wish I had never done it'? Today people are not shouting from the top of the mountain, 'Beware!' They are out there soliciting people for us. They are telling their friends how great it was. Now, they must separate themselves from Christians. Their egos won't allow them to fall to their knees and ask God to forgive them. So they adopt new boundaries. They say, 'People who

say premarital sex is wrong are narrow-minded'. They say, 'It's just another opinion, and

everybody is entitled to their own'."

"Now I understand the saying 'Opinions are like butts. Everybody's got one, and they all stink'. I can see now. With a lofty ego comes an opinion about everything."

"You're getting there."

"When pride is involved, no one can do it quite as good as you."

"Narcissism leaves no doubt who is right."

"I know from experience. Egos need attention. When others are around, there is no swifter way to get attention than to have an opinion about a prevailing topic. A rebel always has a different opinion."

"Rebellion and attention go together like humility and quiet. Rebelling brings shame. Humility brings honor. Continually attracting attention brings ridicule. Quiet, soft-spoken individuals are presumed to be wise."

"So if you just keep your mouth shut, people will assume you are a person with wisdom. No wonder people always laughed at me. I was always trying to impress them. The more I tried, the more the relationship deteriorated. What a fool I was."

"Don't take it so hard. You weren't alone. The majority of the citizenry has been told they can do anything. Apparently, having no boundaries justifies thinking about themselves all the time. You can't put yourself first and be humble. You can't find the answer when all you are thinking about is yourself God's key equation is so simple. One, God first, two, others second. When human beings humble themselves to the point they put God first in their lives and others second, then they stop thinking only about themselves. This changes the dynamics of their lives, and now they focus on others instead of themselves. Most of the sadness we experience is due to dwelling on ourselves. So the fabrications of our thoughts change. Now we are thinking about someone else. This requires the concern be directed away from one's self. To put someone's interest ahead of your own is a wonderful feeling. This is why some people love those years of

parenting. This was the only time they were capable of attending to someone's needs before their own. They didn't know why, they just knew it felt good. They didn't realize it had nothing to do with their biological association with the child. It was simply desiring to put someone before himself or herself. Imagine, they never figured out why they were so content."

"You are the one who tells the truth. So tell me why did I like to drink so much?" I ask.

"Because you never felt like you measured up."

"That's why I drank?"

'Yes. It allowed you to relax. You didn't have to think about your inadequacies. All you had to do was take a drink and your troubles started to slide away.

"What troubles?"

'Come on, you have been doing well. Don't play games with me now. You felt you were inadequate in your work. You always felt you were in over your head. You felt like none of the girls liked you. None of the fellows called you to see if you wanted to go out with the guys. The boss couldn't look at you without a snicker. You were so afraid of being discovered that the only thing you could do was get high. At least then you could kick back and not give a hoot what they thought of you. It sure felt good to feel like that, didn't it, to really not care what they thought? But every morning when you woke up, there you were, the same old guy who ordered that first drink. You see, the beauty to drinking is it doesn't solve anything. This means as long as a person continues to drink, we don't have to worry. It's when they stop they become the problem. Then they take some stupid AA course. They reach out to God and mess everything up. Then they address the real problems they are having and get real solutions for the problems and leave their old buddies behind. As long as they hide their problems by drinking, there is no personal growth. This is exactly what we want."

"If I had quit drinking and looked for some answers, what might I have found?"

'Well, for one thing you might have found that the boss you thought had nothing but contempt for you actually liked you. That snicker was because you had the exact same expressions his younger brother had. He loved and admired his younger brother, who was always getting into something. But you never gave him a chance to get very close to you. You were so afraid he would discover what an idiot you were that you kept your distance. Remember the girl in your apartment building who was beautiful and asked you to go to church with her? Guess what? She went to the same church your boss did. If you had gone to church with her, it would have changed your whole life."

"You mean alcohol did that to me?"

"No. You did that to you. You just used alcohol to make you feel better while you self-destructed. Alcohol and drugs are wonderful. They keep people in a fantasy world. They keep them safely tucked away from the truth. Their world is distorted so they can't find the exit. As long as they are in a world of drugs or alcohol, we can be assured they won't find the truth. God's angels are standing at the doors waiting, but they can't find the doors. It is hard to face the truth. Everyone wants to be accepted. Everyone wants to be loved. Nobody likes rejection. Nobody likes pain. Some days you win, some days the dragon wins. That's life. Some people are so fragile, they can't face the dragon. Those people run for the exit. When you pass through that door of drugs and alcohol, you are safe from the dragon for the time spent behind the door. The only problem is the way to victory is through the dragon. One can never have victory without first facing the dragon."

"What happens if you never face the dragon?"

"You are proof of that. You never faced the dragon, so you never received victory. That's why you are here. You belong to the dragon."

"Oh, that dragon?"

"Are you listening'?"

"Yes. I understand. All those times I thought the people who kept their mouths shut were either cowards or lacked communication skills. This was a big mistake on my part. These were the people who were fighting the dragon. They were practicing self-control. So when everybody was giving their opinion on a subject, even though they may feel strongly about the issue, they were keeping their mouth shut. When we were tearing the boss down and they would speak up for him, they were being honest. They didn't care if they were popular. They didn't have to be seen. They were just living their lives the way God told them to. They were reading the Bible and trying to follow it. All this time I thought they were weak."

"They weren't weak. They were God's children. They go unnoticed by the world in the workplace because they are not trying to be the loudest or the smartest or the bravest. They are just trying to walk with the Lord. Most of the workplace doesn't get it. I call them the Compassionate Conquerors. These Tender Titans claim victory over the dragon. This means they cannot be first here on earth. They must let people like you do all the giving of opinions. They must let the others brag. They must let the others go out with the 'beautiful people' and party. Their reward is not on earth. Their reward is they won't be joining us. They will spend eternity where the streets are paved with the purest gold. The gold is so pure you can see through it. There will be no tears, no sorrow."

"What a world that must be. Is there no way I can go back to the old world and try again?" I almost beg.

"No."

"Is there some way I can be forgiven of my sins?"

"No," LIIANSA responds. "It is over for you. You do yourself no good. Regret is of no use to you here. You have only one focus. You must use all of your ability to sway others. It is your only alternative. If you don't choose to enlist others, you will be of no use to our master. This means you must go to the place of desolation."

"Why have you provided me with all this information? Why do I need to know that God really exists? Why not keep me in the dark? What benefit is it to torture me with the truth?"

"These are good questions. I am bound by the truth," says LIIANSA. "The reason you have been given this information is to make you a worthy adversary."

"Why do I need to know how wonderful God is and everyone who goes to heaven will have such a great time?"

"If you don't know the truth, you can't distort it. Our greatest advantage over the masses is ignorance. The genius of our lord, Satan, is unlike the average person, we know the truth. So we can quote them almost anything and they will buy it. The most important thing is the appearance of sincerity. If the people think you are sincere, they will believe you."

"Are you telling me if I make something up about the Bible or God, and it's a lie, people won't go look it up?"

"In most cases it's the last thing they will do. They will believe you or dismiss you based on their gut feeling about your presentation."

"How can that be? Surely the majority of mankind would take the small amount of time to check it out."

"That is not the case. Most people don't check it against the word of God. They may go to someone they know and debate it or ask someone else if they have ever heard of that particular scripture, but 80 percent of the time, they never look it up. Before the Bible was translated into easy reading, almost no one read it for information. Now we have these Bibles that anyone can understand. You would think that everyone would read them now. This is not true. For some readers, this has saved them. Now, they have a good understanding of God's word. Still, most refuse to read it for themselves. They would prefer to debate the issues with others using their intellect to try and out reason the other. We are in an era much like it was in the

Apostle Paul's time. He went to Athens where he found all the brilliant philosophers standing around debating the different religions and missing the truth. Today's world is the same. The people would rather have a great philosophic discussion about religion than read God's word and accept it as the truth."

"Why would they not read the Bible, and discover the truth for themselves?"

"Did you?"

"No. So what does that mean?"

"Like yourself, most people of today, like in Paul's day, have been reared in homes where there was a Bible sitting on a shelf in the same room with them. The problem is, no one ever got it out and opened it up. So you have a generation that is not comfortable with the Bible. This is why you didn't look anything up. You didn't have a clue where to look. If someone said the Bible says this or that, how would you refute their clam?"

"You're right! I wouldn't know where to look."

"So, like you, they just get that 'deer in the headlight' look when someone is quoting the Bible. People who are considered know-it-alls love to look up things in the Bible. This way they are almost never to be challenged. What a wonderful way to be able to spout off, and everyone listens. No one can prove otherwise, unless of course someone in the group grew up in a strong Christian-based home. The know-it-all quickly changes the subject. Knowing the odds of a someone knowing the Bible at the next social would be rare."

"Is that truly the condition of the world?"

LIIANSA smiles. "Until just recently, the Catholics didn't read the Bible. They were content to believe whatever the priest said. They were on a need-to-know basis. The priest would determine what they needed to know. The problem is those easy-to-read Bibles have worked their way into the Catholic Church, too."

"So how is that a problem?"

"They are becoming more well read. They know the Bible better than the masses in any other time. But they are still lazy, just like all the rest of your society. This means they only read what they feel they must. This gives us the chance to deceive them. If you have only a vague understanding or recall of something, it is easy to misrepresent it. Our greatest challenge comes from someone who is familiar with God's word and is quick to look up anything that sounds the least bit suspicious. This makes it very difficult to pervert God's word. In Colossians 2:8, Paul said,

> "*Don't let others spoil your faith and joy with their philosophies, their wrong and shallow answers built on men's thoughts and ideas, instead of on what Christ has said. For in Christ there is all of God in a human body; so you have everything when you have Christ, and you are filled with God through your union with Christ. He is the highest Ruler, with authority over every other power.*

"How do we encounter someone well versed?'

"The only tool we have is to misinterpret the meaning of His word. The great misinterpreters have one thing in common. They all select a sentence or paragraph that can be easily misconstrued, then taint the meaning. Even those who know the Bible can get confused when there isn't a Bible handy. There are some so good at their craft they can even give the average person a Bible and point to the verse and still beguile their audience."

"That requires some talent!"

"This is what the Dark Angel saw in you. He felt you possessed the skills to achieve these goals. Is he right? Do you posses these abilities?"

"Yes," I answer. "The problem is motivation. When I knew nothing of the truth, I was eager to sin. I enjoyed doing all the wrong things. Now that you have shown me the truth, well, it seems to have had a contrasting effect. Maybe this is temporary. I don't quite know what to say. I feel like I am on the wrong team. I just keep thinking that everything down here is a lie. If everything we do is to deceive and mislead, then maybe when you tell me there is no way I can get to heaven, it's not true. Maybe I can still refuse to be a part of this and get in the back door."

LIIANSA's look is changing. "At least you have the heart of a pure rebel. You couldn't follow when you were on earth, and you can't follow now. This is an inauspicious response. I must tell you, I have asked for the Dark Angel's ruling. This will only take a moment."

"Wait! I'm sure this will pass. It's…just so difficult to comprehend."

LIIANSA speaks. "The Dark Angel is unavailable at the moment. He will see you soon."

"Please wait! I just need some time to think about it."

"My interim has ended. The Dark Angel will govern your fate."

At this moment LIIANSA vanishes.

"Wait! Wait! Please don't go! I am not a rebel. The fact is, I have lost my will to be rebellious. What must I do? Where do I turn? What can come of this? Am I doomed? Will the Dark Angel crush me? Will I be given another chance? Do I want another chance? What am I saying?"

Man, what are they going to do to me? What if everything they told me is a lie? What if there is hope? Maybe I can get out of this place. What would I have to do? Certainly this is not all in vain? Surely someone can hear me, someone who can see my predicament. Definitely someone can rescue me. What must I do? Where do I turn? There has to be a way out of this dilemma! I know! I've got it! Why didn't I think of it before! I drop to my knees. "Father in heaven, I know I have lived a life filled with sin. I ask you to forgive me of my sins now and rescue me from this place. Lift me up and withdraw me from this torment, I pray."

The area seems dismal. There is the feeling of hopelessness. An eerie sensation is everywhere. You can sense the satanic power in the atmosphere. There is no doubt something is present. The area starts to darken. There is a silence that is so profound, it is immeasurable. Suddenly the Dark Angel appears! As he enters the area, there is a roaring sound all around him. I can't see him. He is like a shadow of something. I know it's a being, but I can't make out what it is. The sound is painful—not unbearable, but painful. It is hard to look directly at him. Even though it is dark all around him, when I try to look at him, it's like a radiant light. I just have to turn away. I can tell he is probing my mind. Must think of how I can serve him. He can envision my every thought. What does this mean?

"Please allow me a chance to be an Eluder. I know I can do a good job," I beg. Abruptly he is gone. There is no sign of him. Man! Does this mean I am going to be an

Eluder? Can it be? Did I get my ugly self out of that? Bring it on. That was as close as I ever want to come to a Dark Angel. Boy, was I quaking in my boots. I think I need a drink. No, I need to get out of this place.

A noise, and here are RZLA (the Kerubic Angel) and his three companions flying in to the area. They are looking at me. Oh sh—now a lake just appears out of nowhere. Up from the water comes TAAD (another Kerubic Angel) and his three companions. They, too, are looking at me. Through the walls of the area come BOZA (Kerubic Angel) and his three companions who just happen to be looking at me. Can it get any worse than this? Immediately a tremendous fire bursts out in the area, and out of the fire comes DOPA (you guessed it, Kerubic Angel) and three companions (concluding the Kerubic Angels). Guess who they are looking at? I am moving back very slowly. I am sure of one thing. All hell is going to break loose. These guys don't like each other, and I don't want to be in the way when the conflict starts.

I never saw a Kerubic Angel this close before. Man, they are ugly. The look in their eye is one of pure savagery. They have a forehead like King Kong, a mouth like a baboon. Their arms and chests are like well-developed men, only larger; so are their legs. Their hands have huge fingers, but on the ends, instead of fingernails, they have talons. The same is true of their feet, only the talons are short and thick, as spikes on a football shoe that were ground to a point. Their feet are like those of a lion, but without hair. They move much faster than a man. The RZLA group has larger wings and seems to move as a bird by using their wings to help them move around. They also have skin that almost resembles feathers. The TAAD group has wings that when they were coming out of the water looked as if they were using them as a turtle uses his flippers to move through the water. Their skin is scaly like an alligator's. They also have a tail, and none of the other groups do. The Boza group has the best-developed legs. They seem to leap almost like a frog when moving around. Their wings are smaller than the others. They, too, have scales, but look more like a snake. The DOPA group appears to have skin that looks like metal, almost a dirty bronze. They have a sheen to their skin when they first come out of the fire. The longer they are out of the fire, the more their skin looks like bronze starting to tarnish. Holy—! They can actually exhale fire. ADOP just toasted DTAA. They are snarling at each other. Man! Oh, my God! He is coming over here. 1 must get out! There is nowhere to go! I can't get away! They are all coming toward me!

Terrible screams, screams that have never been heard on earth! There is no description for what these maniacal species are doing. The horror of what is taking place is so unmerciful, I can only look away.

Time passes.

Now I can see I'm not going to make it. The pain is constant. In spite of all that has happened to me, I think I am finally getting it. When the Bible refers to the flesh, it is referring to our flesh, it is referring to our emotions. Survival dictates we are all self-serving; therefore, we are continuously looking for people, places, and things that make us feel good. Given the choice, we would all choose to be happy versus sad. So to be emotionally content or happy, and no other factors in play, we adopt the "If it feels good, do it" philosophy. Why wouldn't you? The whole point to life is to get the most out of it. To live life to its fullest. This is how I lived my life. I felt like I could do anything I wanted as long as I didn't break the law.

Now I know that isn't true. Once you give your life to God, your life changes. Now you have a set of rules to live by. These rules don't go along with your emotions. Your emotional instincts tell you that you come first. God's word says God first and others second. This creates a contrast within your very being. When you read the word of God, in your heart you know it's true. You don't want to believe it, but you know it's true.

What to do? Do you give up your emotional instincts and follow the word? Do you adopt some of the word and try to make some changes in your life without totally redefining yourself? Should you abandon your old self and adopt a new self to adhere to the word of God?

It appears there is only one answer that will do. You must abandon your old lifestyle, and as the Bible says, "You must die to your old self and be reborn." I now understand. What this means is I must give up my emotional instincts and develop self-control. Self-control is bringing your emotions into check. No more "what feels good." but "what is good."

The problem for most is to find out what is right and what is wrong. This is spelled out for you in the Bible. Now that you have the book that contains the laws, all you have to do is follow them. So when your emotions say, "I want that dessert" or "I want the last word" or "I want her or him," you go to the book of life and see what it says. It's that simple. If you follow the rules in the book, you get eternal life. If you follow your emotions and have the dessert, the last word, or unmarried sex, you will spend eternity here in hell.

The children whose parents taught them self-discipline are in good stead. They have a great advantage. They already know how to control their emotions. Those who were allowed to have their own way must now suffer. You will suffer considerably if you are going to bring your emotions under control as an adult. If you don't, you will pay the ultimate price here with us. I can assure you the practice of self-control can't compare to the pain you will feel here. If only I could have one more chance! If only God would hear my plea. So many years of emptiness. So many years of asking questions like, "Why am I here?" "What is this all about?" "Is this all there is?" Now I know! The answers were always right there. There was a Bible within my reach almost every time I asked one of those questions. However, now it is too late.

No, no, not VSNARDA. Nowhere to run. I don't have the strength to move aside. I am helpless. God! His piercing talons are puncturing my ribs and my bowels. We are starting our descent downward to the place of desolation. Now I understand why they called me Pervert. My life was a perversion of God's holy word. I realize now that God provided me with the opportunity. I made my own choices. I could have accepted God's word or rejected it. I chose to reject it. I chose to turn my back on God. Now He has turned His back on me just as He said He would.

Anyone with ears, listen to me. Don't come to this place! Run from sin! Do what is necessary to avoid this place! Live a life that is pleasing to God. Be humble. Do not become prideful. Stay away from all kinds of sin. While there is still life left in you, while there is still hope, ask God to forgive you of your sins. Remember, you must ask it in Jesus' name. Then change your life. Find a church family and become a part of the family of God. Honor Him every day and in everything you do. You might say, "I can't do that," but remember, all things are possible through God. Once you have turned your back on God, He will turn his back on you. But there is still hope! Call on Him.

The pain is growing. I can barely speak.

To have a relationship with the Almighty, you must speak to Him (through prayer) and you must listen to Him (read the Bible). You must do this every day, so no one can separate you from God. Believe me! You don't want to come here! This is real. This is forever. Prison on earth doesn't hold a candle to this. There is no escape. There is no hope. Only pain. As my final act, let it be one of kindness. I beseech you, don't become careless. Don't think there is time for you don't know when your name appears in the book of life, as through on earth. Turn to God while there is time!

As we approach the place of desolation, the screams are growing louder and louder. I—can—no—longer—speak….